**SECOND LANGUAGE ACQUISITION**
Series Editor: David Singleton, *Trinit*

C000092822

# Silence in Second Language Learning

## A Psychoanalytic Reading

SUPPLIED BY COUTTS U.K

## Colette A. Granger

**MULTILINGUAL MATTERS LTD**
Clevedon • Buffalo • Toronto • Sydney

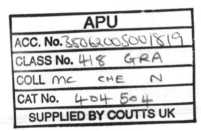

**APU**

ACC. No. 38062005001819

CLASS No. 418 GRA

COLL mc CHE N

CAT No. 404 504

**SUPPLIED BY COUTTS UK**

**Library of Congress Cataloging in Publication Data**
Granger, Colette A.
Silence in Second Language Learning: A Psychoanalytic Reading
Colette A. Granger – 1st edn.
Second Language Acquisition: 6
Includes bibliographical references and index.
1. Second language acquisition. 2. Silence. 3. Psychoanalysis.
I. Title. II. Second language acquisition
P118.2.G734 2004
418--dc21           2003008651

**British Library Cataloguing in Publication Data**
A catalogue entry for this book is available from the British Library.

ISBN 1-85359-698-1 (hbk)
ISBN 1-85359-697-3 (pbk)

**Multilingual Matters Ltd**
*UK*: Frankfurt Lodge, Clevedon Hall, Victoria Road, Clevedon BS21 7HH.
*USA*: UTP, 2250 Military Road, Tonawanda, NY 14150, USA.
*Canada*: UTP, 5201 Dufferin Street, North York, Ontario M3H 5T8, Canada.
*Australia*: Footprint Books, PO Box 418, Church Point, NSW 2103, Australia.

Copyright © 2004 Colette A. Granger.

All rights reserved. No part of this work may be reproduced in any form or by any means without permission in writing from the publisher.

Typeset by Wordworks Ltd.
Printed and bound in Great Britain by the Cromwell Press Ltd.

*To my family*

# Contents

# Foreword

I was recently involved in the assessment and translation into French of a medical questionnaire for an international organisation specialising in epidemiology. A whole morning had been earmarked for the task, more than long enough, the organisers believed, to deal with forty short items. We started on Item 1 dead on nine with brisk enthusiasm and by our one o'clock lunchtime ... we were still on Item 1. This asked respondents to agree or disagree with the following statement:

*I like who I am.*

There we were, a committee made up of specialists in an extremely wide and imposing range of disciplines – medicine and translation, statistics and ethnolinguistics, sociology and psychology – completely floored by an utterance that contains only five words, all of them monosyllabic and amongst the commonest words in the language. And the really awful bit, the bit that had us avoiding eye contact with one another, drinking too much coffee and hoping it was fire-drill day, was that not only could we not translate it, we could not even understand *why* we could not translate it. Even worse, whilst we all thought we understood it, no one could say what it meant.

Reactions to this state of affairs varied. One colleague exclaimed, 'That expression is *so* American!', which obviously explained matters to his own satisfaction. Another invocated the name of Descartes. A third wondered if thirty-nine questions wasn't enough, really? We had run head-on into an epistemological labyrinth and could not find our way out, our shouts only echoing endlessly off the walls. Even those who were able to accept the idea of cultural variation in concepts of personhood at some highly generalised theoretical level had great difficulty in believing that this could result in such particularised differences in *self*-expression, that such a simple phrase could be so difficult.

It is these issues, the relationships between language and identity, between languages and the architecture of the psyche, between the individual and the ineffable, that are addressed in this remarkable book.

*Silence in Second Language Learning* is an insightful, original and important work. It is insightful because it brings together two seemingly disparate topics – *identity* and *the silent period* – and shows that they are related in a profound and systematic way. It is original because, starting from this unusual juxtaposition of topics, it formulates questions that have not been asked elsewhere, calling on work in different disciplines – linguistics, psychoanalysis, social psychology, anthropology and language didactics – and weaving them into a cogently-argued synthesis. To do so requires an exceptionally wide and genuinely interdisciplinary intellectual and methodological framework, qualities that Colette Granger displays with brio whilst at the same time managing to remain readable: even when she is dealing with complex and demanding issues, she does so in a clear, energetic style in which opinions and arguments are expressed firmly, but where there is no trace of stridency. Alternative views are examined and given a fair hearing. The reader is in the presence of an inquiring and well-stocked mind whose enthusiasm is always tempered by reason.

And *Silence in Second Language Learning* is important for two main reasons:

- Firstly, there is a widespread perception that most countries in the world are going through various forms of identity crisis as a result of globalisation, cataclysmic political and social shifts, and ideological and religious realignments. Identities are being reconfigured at every level: national and international, regional and local, individual. Such developments always have linguistic repercussions of one kind or another, yet they have received relatively little attention in applied linguistics or language didactics (as opposed to anthropology and ethnology).
- Secondly, in applied linguistics circles, the expression '(the identity of) the learner' is in fact a misnomer: it is not about the individual identity (the self and social person, roles and ethos ... date of birth, beliefs, occupation, tastes, etc.) of a single incorporated person. In applied linguistics discourse, 'the learner' is an abstraction, a generalised representation of the *learning process.* Colette Granger's book tries to remedy this reductionism by focusing on the individual, 'the learning, speaking individual'.

In outline, three basic premises lie at the heart of this study. Firstly, Colette Granger contends that there are aspects of language learning and acquisition that are psychical in nature. Secondly, she contends that the silent period, an objectively observable stage in the development of some second language learners, is a manifestation of those psychical characteristics and their functioning. And thirdly, she argues that psychoanalytical theory can provide the conceptual and methodological tools necessary to identify, describe and investigate the problems and processes involved. If 'identity' and a sense of self are constructed in and through an internal monologue or, rather, an intrapersonal dialogue, what happens when the language being used changes, as is the case of a second language learner? How can I talk to my self properly in a language I do not yet master?

What groups of readers might be interested in reading *Silence in Second Language Learning*? My answers, in no particular order, would be:

- Thoughtful and reflective teachers who wish better to understand their learners and their own role in the learning process and *vis à vis* their learners. Moreover, in classroom terms at least, learner identity cannot be examined separately from teacher identity, since their roles are complementary. Teachers hungry for a humanistic appraisal of their own identities and roles – and there are quite a few of them, I believe – will find much of interest here. And, of course, teachers are often people who have as learners themselves been through the types of experience discussed here.
- People interested in psychoanalysis whether professionally or not: the professionals for the originality of the topic, others for its accessibility.
- People interested in the processes of language learning and acquisition. The silent period is an intriguing phenomenon in itself, of course, and this is an effective, critical synthesis of much work in second language acquisition, social psychology and discourse analysis. Again, this is an under-researched topic, as are the emergence and social construction of the self and identity, especially in bi- or multilingual settings.
- People interested in identity: this is a surprisingly large group, given the intense interest in identity in anthropology, sociology and politics.

I am sure that *Silence in Second Language Learning* will have a *succès d'estime:* I very much hope it will also have the other types of success it richly deserves, since it represents a major and welcome shift of perspective on language learning and 'the learner'.

*Philip Riley*
*C.R.A.P.E.L. (Centre de Recherches et*
*d'Applications Pédagogiques en Langues)*
*Université Nancy 2,*
*France*

# Acknowledgements

Interdisciplinarity is a tricky thing – to engage distinct discourses in a theoretical conversation is to ask of the reader a kind of indulgence. This book, which is about learning, has benefited from some fine teachers, whose diverse intellectual passions have encouraged, and indulged, my own. I am thankful to Alice Pitt, who introduced me to psychoanalytic theory at exactly the right moment, and who continues to strengthen my engagement with it through thoughtful enquiry and patient humour. I also thank Heather Lotherington for her enthusiastic response to my initial idea, and for her linguistic insights at different points during this project. Early on I received some useful bibliographic suggestions from Kathleen Bailey: I am grateful to her, as well as to Barbara Godard and Sandra Schecter for their attentive reading and provocative questioning of my work at later stages. To Philip Riley, whose response to and suggestions for the manuscript have been most generous and helpful, I owe a particular debt of thanks.

Others have contributed to my thinking through their writing and in conversation. Among these are Deborah Britzman, Mary Leigh Morbey, and my colleagues in the doctoral programme in the Faculty of Education at York University, in particular Chloë Brushwood-Rose, Trent Davis, John Ippolito, Sara Matthews and Karleen Pendleton-Jiménez. Peggy Warren, in the Scott Library at York, has provided important bibliographic assistance, and the staff of the Resource Sharing Department, especially Gladys Fung, Julie Pippo and Samantha McWilliams, have performed, more times than I can remember, the magic of obtaining hard-to-find texts in record time.

One of the delights of any journey is that, whether or not the destination is known, there are unexpected moments at each bend in the road. For me there have been many such moments. One was given to me by Dale Smith, whose observation of a silent kindergarten pupil was one of the seeds that grew into this work, and another came from Ronald Conrad, who suggested many years ago that I could write. I thank them both.

The following publishers have kindly granted permission to reproduce copyright material: W.W. Norton & Company, Inc. for passages from *Inhibitions, Symptoms, and Anxiety* by Sigmund Freud, translated by Alix Strachey; Dutton (a division of the Penguin Group, USA, Inc.) for material from *Lost in Translation* by Eva Hoffman; and Pantheon Books (a division of Random House, Inc.) for material from *Beast in the Nursery* by Adam Phillips.

Finally, I owe a sincere debt to those I love: to my children, Paul and Emma, for their love and for the reminder that it's a good thing to read a recipe book, too, once in a while; to Manuel and Martin for generously sharing their father and their computer; to my friends for the gifts of companionship, laughter and encouragement that endure over time and distance; and to Alberto Mendelzon, whose affection, intelligence and humour give pleasure to my work and to my life.

## Introduction

# Silence in Second Language Learning: A Present Absence

> One does not inhabit a country; one inhabits a language.
> That is our country, our fatherland – and no other.
> Émile M. Cioran
> *Anathemas and Admirations*, 1986

> A five-year-old child newly arrived in Toronto, whose first language is
> not English, attends his all-English kindergarten for several months
> without speaking. The teacher tries hard to interest him in the brightly
> coloured building blocks and other toys, art materials and books, but he
> remains passive, distant, silent. His silence is disturbing. His teacher is
> concerned, but she is also wise: she waits. Then one day the class takes a
> trip to the zoo. In the section devoted to reptiles, the boy spots a
> reticulated python, wrapped several times around a branch inside a
> large, glass-fronted display case. The boy darts over to his teacher, grabs
> her hand tightly and pulls her hard, insistently, away from her
> conversation with another student, over to the glass case. He points at
> the python and shouts, over and over, 'Me know this! Me know this!
> This my home, teacher, this my home!'
> Dale Smith
> Personal communication, 1997

When the story of that young child's awakening into English was first
related to me by his teacher, I wondered how she might have felt when,
after months of silence, her student finally began to speak. I was curious
about how the child himself might have felt, speaking out for the first time
in a new language. But most of all I wanted to think about the meaning of
the period during which the child had not spoken: his months of silence.
How did he live? What was he doing? Who, indeed, was he?

This study grew out of that curiosity. My original intention was to
interrogate the experience of that boy, and others like him, who dwell for a
time in the solitary space between a first and a second language. I wanted to
articulate my curiosity about a component of the highly complex and indi-
vidualised process of second language acquisition (SLA)[1] – a phenomenon
referred to by linguists as the silent period, and generally defined as a span
of time of varying length, during which some beginning second language

1

(L2) learners do not willingly produce the language they are learning. This silent period, so described, parallels to a substantial degree the first year or so of life prior to the beginning of speech in the mother tongue. During this time, according to Rod Ellis, 'children go through a lengthy period of listening to people talk to them before they produce their first words' (Ellis, 1996: 82). The pre-production stage of the first-language learner is distinguished from the L2 silent period both by cognitive development and by physiology. Ellis (1996: 82) writes that in the first language a 'silent period is necessary, for the young child needs to discover what language is and what it does'. The vocal apparatus also has to develop sufficiently for language production. By contrast, in second language acquisition the development of the physical apparatus has been achieved, and a language (and therefore, presumably, some knowledge *about* language) has been acquired.

My wish was to explore the question of whether the silent period might also be a psychological phenomenon, a non-linguistic as well as a linguistic step in the continuous process of self-concept formation and re-formation. But mostly I wanted to try to foreground the relationship between individual identity and self-concept, as expressed in and by the silent period, and the process of second language acquisition. Words and worlds are threads woven together into the fabric of lived experience: what happens, I wondered, when they become unravelled?

The first thing that happened, and it happened quite early on, was that my own tidy little wish came undone. First, I was surprised to discover that, while a number of reasons have been offered by way of explanation for this stage of L2 acquisition (Larsen-Freeman & Long, 1991; Lightbown & Spada, 1996; Saville-Troike, 1988), one of its most striking features is that it does not seem to occur in all learners. Moreover, when it does occur it varies, in degree and in duration. The silent period is more idiosyncratic than I had imagined, and consequently not as clearly conceptualised or described as I had anticipated. Indeed, so variable is it that, in contrast with its apparent equivalent, the necessary and universal pre-verbal period in first language acquisition, Ellis describes it as 'not obligatory', since an second language learner 'already knows about language' (1996: 82). And linguistic research bears out this conceptualisation of a silent period as a typical, yet nevertheless variable and non-universal, occurrence in second language acquisition (Gibbons, 1985; Naiman *et al.*, 1978; Saville-Troike, 1988).

The idiosyncrasy of the silent period suggests that the numerous phenomena that second language acquisition (SLA) research groups in the category 'silent period', and perhaps even the concept of silence writ large, are not quite transparent. The question asks itself: precisely what might it signify that a stage in a learning process is not obligatory? In this particular context, what does it mean to say that the previous acquisition of a first language renders a silent period unnecessary in the learning of a second? If it is truly redundant for an individual who already 'knows about language', given that such knowledge is by definition a necessary precondition to second language acquisition, no second language learner should ever undergo a silent period. And yet many do – perhaps more than we know or can readily determine. Depending on the definition applied (and specifically on the lack of consensus about how long or short a period of silence should be to constitute a 'silent period' as such), it can be argued that *all* second language learners go through a pre-production period that might, again depending on definition, be labelled a silent period.

In the light of the position I take in this study, namely that silence in second language acquisition is a much larger phenomenon than what is named the silent period, these questions, however interesting, are not central. And so, taking at face value, for the moment, Ellis's assessment of the silent period as non-obligatory, I surmise that knowledge of a first language is a necessary, but perhaps not a sufficient, condition for the elimination of a silent period in second language learning. That it occurs at all, however idiosyncratically, must therefore be attributable, at least in part, to something else.

As well as being a series of intra-personal cognitive stages, SLA is without doubt also a social process. It takes place within the individual, certainly, but that individual is moving at all times through a world populated, and articulated linguistically, by others. In the case of the second language learner, that world and its population may differ in many ways from the environment in which the first language was acquired. Such differences might well impose on the learner demands that are new, complex, and even – in ways that are social as well as linguistic – incomprehensible.

But first language acquisition is a social process too. Even the Chomskyan (1972) view of an innate capacity for language does not claim that language development is possible in the complete absence of social contact. In fact, the cognitive work that Ellis (1996: 82) refers to as the discovery of 'what language is and what it does' can take place only in an environment where language is present and available to be discovered. From the perspective of language as a social phenomenon, then, might there be fewer, or different, reasons for a silent period in the acquisition of a second language than in the acquisition of a first?

The silent period, along with its unpredictability, is a troubling issue, not only for linguists but also for educators. Given that they often encounter second-language learners (whether by design in the case of second language instruction, or by accident when a student's mother tongue is not the language of instruction), it follows that teachers too, at least from time to time, find themselves confronted by the silence of the second-language learner. What are they to do? How are they to understand this silence – as cognitive or affective, desirable or problematic, deliberate or unconscious, guileless or manipulative? How might they respond to it? And how might they engage with it pedagogically? To explore these questions is part of the work of this study. Yet to begin such an exploration involves asking what purpose the silent period might serve: what precisely is silence in second language acquisition, and what is that silence being used by the learner to do?

Like the methodological problems in SLA research, some of which I will enumerate below, the complexities of an individual's experience as an second-language learner – and the difficulties of interpreting that experience and the silence within it – arise at least in part out of two interrelated issues. First, neither language acquisition nor the study of it is a tidy process. There is a kind of muddiness inherent both in the research methods in question and in the subject (that is, the topic) under investigation, which is not easily explained – or 'researched' – away. Relatedly, this muddiness arises, I propose to a significant extent, out of a widespread tendency to overlook or avoid another element – another 'subject' –that may be messier and more complex than either language learning or language research and that to me seems crucial to the assessment of individual differences in language acquisition. This element is the learning, speaking (and at times silent), individual. More specifically, it is that individual's self, or self-concept, which remains unnamed in at least two ways: first by SLA research which, to a substantial degree, floats on the already-cloudy surface of personality rather than diving into the murkier depths below; and second by the subject him- or herself, the language learner who, as I will argue later, simply cannot do the naming. The problem becomes how to study something that linguistics describes and measures, that pedagogy (both in practice and in theory) often perceives as an empty phenomenon, that the individual subject cannot explain despite – or because of – being immersed in it, and that 'common sense' denies has importance at all.

Moreover, as a focus of study, the silent period in the context of second language learning (and silence qua silence in any context) is inherently problematic. After all, whether transparent or not, whether informed by prior knowledge or not, whether obligatory or not, it is by definition, in some sense at least, silent. And in Western cultures whose naturalised,

common-sense operating principles favour performance over contempla-
tion, participation over inaction, and – what is most relevant here – speech
over silence, there is something peculiar, even counter-intuitive, about
investigating something that in a sense is not there. It is a struggle to recon-
struct silence, not as an absence, an emptiness that must be filled with
something else in order to be meaningful, but rather as an investigable
actuality. Nevertheless, this is the position I take: that, however counter-
intuitive it might seem, the 'emptiness' of silence within second language
learning is imagined and not real. For, just as silence is part of language
itself, encoded and unencoded, lying both within and outside speech at the
levels of phonology, syntax and discourse, as well as in the sense that
begins to approach what I am addressing here, of 'things not said' (Schmitz,
1994), silence in general and the silent period in particular are significant
aspects of second language acquisition.

If there is more to the silent period than the mere absence of speech, there
is also a sense in which something seems to be absent from linguistics'
explanations of it. Where SLA research disappoints, in my view, is in its
reluctance to recognise adequately and explore deeply the multiple non-
linguistic levels on which L2 acquisition functions. Here I am not referring
only to aspects or characteristics such as age, gender, motivation, attitudes
or learning styles, which have certainly been named, counted, categorised,
defined and described in various and often useful ways. As well as
listening for 'things not said', my aim is to consider the subjective experiences of some of the persons who are 'not saying' those things. The term
*personality*, which is commonly put forward both as comprising such traits
as self-esteem, affect, anxiety, extroversion and motivation (Brown, 1994a;
Naiman *et al*, 1978), and as informing choices made by learners in some
circumstances (Harder, 1980), perhaps comes closest to what I want to
examine, but even it is not quite adequate. Rather, just as linguistics itself,
for example, distinguishes between surface and deep structures of syntax,
such that surface structure is based on what lies, metaphorically, beneath it,
so I seek to look at deeper aspects of individuals, aspects that ground the
'surface structures' of self-esteem, extroversion and personality in general.
And this goal invites, again, that more fundamental question: what is the
significance of silence in the process of learning to speak?

My second and more daunting discovery, in addition to the idiosyncratic aspects of the silent period itself, was this: just as there is more to the
silent period than a mere absence of speech, silence itself within the second
language acquisition process is a much larger phenomenon, and more
multifaceted, than the silent period as such. For example, Ron Scollon and
Suzanne Scollon's study of interethnic communication (Scollon & Scollon,

1981) offers a clear and helpful comparison between the ways in which Athabaskan and English speakers perceive one another with respect to silence and speech. And in *Perspectives on Silence*, Deborah Tannen and Muriel Saville-Troike gather together the writing of authors who illuminate quite diverse ways of thinking about and interpreting various kinds of silence (Tannen & Saville-Troike, 1985). Within that collection, George Saunders' work on the use of 'noise and silence ... as stylised strategies' for management of emotions (Saunders, 1985: 165), Gregory Nwoye's examination of numerous socially and individually negotiated ritual and ceremonial silences among the Igbo people of Nigeria (Nwoye, 1985), and a discussion of 'the silent Finn' by Jaakko Lehtonen and Kari Sajavaara (Lehtonen & Sjavaara, 1985: 193) point to multiple, culturally-organised meanings and valuations of silence. The Tannen and Saville-Troike volume also includes Emma Muñoz-Duston and Judith Kaplan's highly useful annotated listing of works, originating in fields as diverse as sociolinguistics, religion and business, that interpret silence as 'ranging from hesitation phenomena ... to nonverbal communication' (Muñoz-Duston & Kaplan, 1985: 235).

The literature on these multiple uses and functions of silence is highly interesting and significant, but it is not my precise focus in this book. Rather, I am interested in reading silence within the second language acquisition process less as an interpretable communicative strategy and more as a manifestation of identity-formation processes (which consist of intra- and interpersonal components), though the two are, of course, not unrelated. To me, it is as if the learner's psychical state, specifically that individual's self-concept, functions as a kind of cloth woven out of the threads of all the mutually-informing phenomena (such as learning style, cognitive and social factors, and personality) that help to shape the rate and degree of an individual's success in second language acquisition. To investigate either those individual threads or the final garment (the person who has moved, to whatever degree of success, through the second language acquisition process) without examining the cloth itself and the tearing, fraying and re-stitching to which it might be subjected by the process of SLA, would be to neglect a central aspect of that process.

The question of silence is interesting merely for the fact that it is concomitant and apparently crucial to the process for some, but not all, second-language learners. But it is even more interesting, and I argue more important, for what it might articulate despite, or indeed through, its apparent lack of expression. I hold that what silence signifies could actually be much more than the absence of speech during the process of second language acquisition, that it may be a psychical moment, as well as a linguistic stage, in the complex process of moving from one language to another, and from one *self* to another. For silence is not limited to the absence of verbal expression. The self, the identity, can also be silent, unexpressed, and even – at least temporarily – lost. Further, the experience of a silenced self, which can occur in a shift from one linguistic identity to another, is not limited to individuals taking up a new life in a new country: I recall the story of a student who, having withdrawn from a French immersion class, said that he felt as if part of his identity had been removed (Gillis, 1999, personal communication). Neither is the experience limited to the acquisition of a second language. A six-year-old child attending a Grade 1 class near Toronto, who had learned English (her mother tongue) in Jamaica, confided to me that she felt 'like nothing' when her teacher (also Anglophone but born in Canada) made her pronounce, over and over, the words 'the' and 'thank you' because, said the teacher, the girl's pronunciation of the digraph *th* was 'wrong'.

The title of this introduction is suggested by a passage in Shoshana Felman's book *What Does a Woman Want? Reading and Sexual Difference,* in which she engages 'the nameless *I* who, present as an absence, is the bearer of the silence and the speech of [Virginia Woolf's] *A Room of One's Own* and who ... is speaking insofar as she is *voiceless*, executed, dead' (Felman, 1993: 45; italics in original). The voicelessness to which Felman refers is linked to her argument that 'none of us, as women, has as yet, precisely, an autobiography'. She maintains that this lack is a consequence of women's having been socialised 'to see ourselves as objects and to be positioned as the Other, estranged to ourselves ... ' (Felman, 1993: 14). If, as Felman puts forward, an individual needs a life story – an autobiography – in order to have a voice, and if, conversely, she must have a voice with which to tell that life story, what can it mean to have a voice and a language, and then, if not to lose the voice literally, to find oneself, nevertheless, quite outside the language, exiled from its power to tell? Might it be like losing one's own story altogether, like having a 'room of one's own' but misplacing the key that opens the door to that room? While Felman is describing a voicelessness that differs in quality and in context from that of the second-language learner, whom I regard as caught between two languages and therefore not located in or held by either, there is, I think, something analogous between these two kinds of estrangement. The first is separation from oneself and one's story through sexual difference read as otherness, the second is an otherness to oneself, as well as to one's social environment, that arises from a kind of linguistic homelessness.

To arrive at the recognition that silence in second language learning is a complex and multi-level phenomenon is not, however, to reach any answers. Rather, it is to come upon, and to ask, more questions. Some are methodological. How, precisely, might we begin to examine the silent period this way – as a moment at which it is not just speech, but also the self, the identity, that is silent? How might it be possible to get inside something that common sense tells us is not *something* at all? How can a self that may not be able to name itself tell the story of the not-naming? How, in other words, can we find content, and make meaning, in and from silence? Other questions, naturally, concern the usefulness of such an exploration. What might be the implications of whatever meaning we make of silence? And how might thinking about the silent period in such ways be of use to individuals, whether learners or teachers, engaged in the process of second language acquisition?

My work is, therefore, born of a double paradox: that the *silent period* in the second language acquisition process is not truly silent, and that silence in general, within that process, has a great deal to say. It is rich with significance, but its significance is latent. Indeed, what could be more latent, in terms of the content of language, than silence? My objective is to weave together some of the theoretical threads of linguistics and psychoanalytic thought in an attempt to engage with, and to trouble more deeply, the ways in which silence in second language acquisition, including the silent period, informs and is informed by the messy process of self-construction and self-knowledge with which language is so intimately connected. In asking how thinking about the silent period as an event that is linguistic, social and psychical might be helpful for deepening our understanding of it, I am faced with the same problem as before: how can I listen to what is not said? How can I make silence speak?

The fact of silence in the subjective experience of the second-language learner, and the difficulty of articulating that silence, mirror in a surprising way the apparent silence on the part of much SLA research about the relationship between identity and silence in second language learning. Like Felman's woman, always positioned as 'Other', who cannot get at her own story, neither the second-language learner nor the linguistic research into the experience of that learner can fully access themselves; both are in some sense hidden from themselves. Later, when in an attempt to explore these questions I turn to psychoanalytic theory, which finds value in latent content, this symmetry may gesture at an interesting and helpful way to think about these two different but related silences, but for the present it is sufficient to take notice of their similar rhythms.

To begin, I explore the SLA research itself. Chapter 1 addresses several tasks. First, in order to arrive at working definitions of *silence* and *silent period* for the purposes of my study, I examine the ways in which the two terms are used by different SLA researchers. Next, I discuss some of the work that has been undertaken using these research paradigms, with the goal of understanding the current state of linguistic research into the silent period in particular, and silence as an idiosyncratic aspect of second language acquisition in general. Addressing the peculiar messiness of the terms, and the contradictory aspects inherent in the tricky fact of silence in language, I consider the moment when research into second language acquisition seems effectively to shut down, becoming oddly silent on the subject of silence, and I then venture off in pursuit of a methodology that augments SLA research's more positivist approach.

In the course of that quest, I offer a brief overview of some socially-oriented theories of identity construction and language acquisition. Although these discourses are not my central focus, they offer considerable support for the three contentions that lie at the heart of this study:

- second language acquisition is a process involving psychical as well as linguistic and social elements;
- for some learners silence might be a manifestation of those psychical elements;
- psychoanalytic theory can serve as one among many interpretive frameworks for exploring the phenomenon of silence within the complex process of second language acquisition.

Chapter 2 takes up the question of the learner's subjective experience of silence, aiming to address questions about how selves are created, broken, transformed and remade through the work of language learning, and to think about some of the ways in which silence may implicate, and be implicated in, the process of second language acquisition. To that end, I move from discussing SLA research and social theories of self-construction to engaging psychoanalytic thought in a kind of theoretical conversation that makes connections between SLA research and some of the ideas of Sigmund Freud, Donald Winnicott, Adam Phillips and Jacques Lacan. Grounding my discussion in four overarching concepts central to psycho-analytic theory – anxiety, loss, conflict and ambivalence – I examine these concepts as they might relate, in some learners, to the encounter between the self and the process of second language acquisition.

Chapters 3 and 4 bring together psychoanalytic theory, SLA research, and narrative writing. I begin by asserting my sense of the fit between psychoanalytic theory and narrative analysis, and its usefulness in studying the problem of silence in second language learning. Chapter 3 then turns to an engagement with several autobiographies and memoirs, among them texts by Patrick Chamoiseau, Eva Hoffman, Alice Kaplan and Richard Rodriguez. Here my aim is to use psychoanalytic thought as an interpretive methodology for uncovering the ways in which the texts speak about their authors' silences within the second language learning process, and the ways in which, paradoxically, the narratives are themselves silent. In Chapter 4, I discuss the original aims of language-learner diaries, and my own reckoning about their helpfulness in a study of silence. Then, I examine some diaries written by second-language learners in various settings and circumstances. My goal in this chapter is to explore how these different but related narratives reveal, directly and indirectly, manifestations of the psychoanalytic concepts of anxiety, ambivalence, conflict and loss that I believe might lie at the core of the SLA process in some individuals.

The final chapter addresses some of the connections that individuals make with language and with second language education. Working from the psychoanalytic premise – 'Anna Freud's punch line ... that education can be defined as all types of interference' (Britzman, 1998: 1) – the chapter offers a discussion of some of the specific ways in which silence in second language learning might be understood to interfere with the competing wishes of the many participants in the 'interference that is education'. It continues with a brief examination of some second-language teaching models that seem to have the potential to approach a new pedagogy for which silence might be tolerable, and offers some concluding comments on the implications of such a pedagogy for educational research and for education as a whole.

There is no shortage of writing that relates to and invites connections with the theme of this project. The work of Madeline Ehrman and Zoltán Dörnyei, for example, brings into relation the 'interlocking perspectives ... of the psychotherapist and the educator ... [who both] seek to bring about change in cognitive and emotional processes' (Ehrman & Dörnyei, 1998: 16), and calls on earlier explorations of resistance in learning (Curran, 1972; MacLennan & Dies, 1992; Wolfe & Kolb, 1984) to allude to silence as one of a number of 'particularly powerful forms of resistance' (Ehrman & Dörnyei, 1998: 184). Still, of the authors whose work I engage, those who write from positions within the discipline of psychoanalysis do not, for the most part, work specifically with the topic of silence in second language acquisition. Conversely, those who write as linguists do not consider the phenomenon psychoanalytically. That synthesis, accompanied by the triangulation of narrative texts with these two distinct modes of thought, is my task. Nevertheless, I am struck by how the work of both psychoanalytic theorists and SLA researchers seems to invite a confluence between aspects of their divergent approaches to the problems of identity, language and silence. Simply put, they hint at each other, and my work is the taking up of those hints.

It is a peculiar business, hinting. Psychoanalyst Adam Phillips (1999: 75) takes 'a stab at hinting' as one of the characteristics of psychoanalytic theory and practice. 'After all', writes Phillips, 'not everything may be intended as a hint, but anything might be experienced as one' (Phillips, 1999: 90). He distinguishes, too, between hints, which must be taken freely and out of which something can be made, and orders, which 'can only be submitted to or rejected' (1999: 111). For my part, and for this study, I agree. My work receives hints, often peculiar and compelling, from SLA research, social theories of the construction of the self, and psychoanalytic theory. I take up some of those hints and, although I work most closely with psychoanalytic theory, I do not attempt to categorically supersede any discipline with any other.

Further, because this study deals with some complicated concepts, it seems as important to state at the outset what it does *not* do, in addition to what it does. Thus, I must emphasise that it is not my intention to pathologise either the process of second language acquisition or the phenomenon of silence within that process. I do not adopt the patently erroneous position that second language learning is always and only a negative or subtractive process, whether socially, linguistically or psychically. Nor do I contend that either the second language acquisition process as such or the qualities of the phenomena that may or may not accompany it should – or can – be understood as unvarying. For, like the lives of the individuals engaged in it (the complexity of which will always exceed any single interpretation that can be made of them), each process of second language acquisition is many-layered and influenced by multiple factors: physiological, psychological, environmental and cultural. Thus, for example, I make no claims concerning those individuals, engaged in the process of learning a second language, for whom silence in one of its many forms is not a factor.

Neither do I maintain that there is only one way to understand the concepts of silence or identity that are central to my work, for that too would be quite wrong. With respect to the former, I have mentioned earlier some of the work that has been done on the many socially and culturally grounded uses of silence. And, in a similar vein, as regards identity, in addition to the literature I will review in Chapter 1, which conceptualises identity as a social construction, studies by Signe Howell (1988) and Joanna Overing (1988) are examples of research that offers empirical evidence in support of the view of identity as manifested differently in and through different cultures.

To reiterate, denying or conflating these multiple conceptualisations of identity and silence would be as absurd as insisting that all individuals who acquire a second language experience identical silent periods: I do not wish to do either of these things. What I do want, simply put, is to enquire into the possibility that *for some individuals* the process of second language acquisition, and the revisions of identity that at different moments may accompany that process, might contain echoes (paradoxically articulated through silences that themselves vary in quality), of earlier psychical moments about which psychoanalytic theory has something helpful to say. My desire, then, is to consider notions of silence, identity and language learning in an effort to trouble and to expand them. I anticipate that such a study might function as a kind of prism, allowing the consideration of silence in second language learning, and research about it, from new, often strange and sometimes even surprising angles. And so, in bringing into relation aspects of the disciplines and discourses of psychoanalytic theory, social theories of identity, and linguistics, my goal throughout this work is to complicate rather than compromise them: not to refute or deny the socially and linguistically determined meanings of silence, but rather to add something new to the mix – to enrich, I hope, rather than to simplify.

## Notes

1. A few words on terminology:

(1) *Acquisition/learning*: Stephen Krashen (1985: 1) distinguishes second language *acquisition* – 'a subconscious process identical in all important ways to the process children utilize in acquiring their first language' from *learning* – a conscious process that results in 'knowing about' language. But this differentiation, though influential, has not been universally accepted. For example, while James Gee (1992: 13) similarly differentiates the two processes (describing *acquisition* as subconscious and naturalistic, and *learning* as conscious, usually involving deliberate teaching of some kind, and comprising some metaknowledge), he nevertheless asserts that 'much of what we come by in life ... involves a mixture of acquisition and learning'. Others find the binary distinction itself problematic: Peter Robinson (1996) supports Barry McLaughlin's earlier (1978) contention regarding the difficulty of ascertaining 'whether L2 learners are operating via consciously accessed "rules" or via subconsciously determined intuitions or "feel" in making grammaticality judgments' (Robinson 1996: 7). And Rosamond Mitchell and Florence Myles suggest that what matters most in distinguishing learning from acquisition is the 'difference between meaningful communication ... [and] ... conscious attention to form' (Mitchell & Myles, 1998: 36), and that either of these – or both in combination – can occur equally in naturalistic or institutional settings. Further, as will become evident, the narratives I examine in this study originate in a variety of institutional, non-institutional, and mixed circumstances. While these texts can be understood as bolstering the view of learning and acquisition as overlapping, intermingling processes, my goal is to explore overt and latent articulations of silence in them. I make no definitive claims regarding the relationship, if one exists, between the characteristics of a particular learning/ acquisition context and either the existence or the qualities of silence (though that would surely be an interesting study). Thus, for my purposes, the distinc-

tion between the two terms, learning and acquisition, is not pivotal, and I use them interchangeably.

(2) *Psychological/psychical, self/subject*: Although SLA research tends to favour the use of the term *psychological* to refer to events of mind, or psyche, given my use of psychoanalytic theory as an interpretive framework in this study, I do not here distinguish between *psychological* and *psychical*. Similarly, the terms *self* and *subject* are both used to refer to the individual learner (or acquirer) of language.

*Chapter 1*

# Averting the Gaze: Silence in Second Language Acquisition Research

> *We live inside the act of discourse. But we should not assume that a verbal matrix is the only one in which the articulations and conduct of the mind are conceivable. There are modes of intellectual and sensuous reality founded not on language ... [and] there are actions of the spirit rooted in silence. It is difficult to speak of these, for how should speech justly convey the shape and vitality of silence?*
> George Steiner
> *The Retreat from the Word*, 1970

> *Even silence speaks.*
> Hausa proverb

## Defining Silence

The problem of silence in second language acquisition begins with a problem of language itself, specifically a question of meaning: what is silence, and more precisely what is the silent period, within the second language acquisition process? The terms are not as transparent, nor is the question as easily answered, as they at first appear. There are clues within SLA research itself about the elusiveness of the silent period as a subject of study, but second language research has reached no clear consensus on the more specific issue of the meaning of the term *silent period*, or on the larger question of what actually constitutes silence in the context of second language acquisition. This lack of consensus has the potential to be problematic for, while difference among different researchers is not unusual – since research, like much of human endeavour, is an interpretive act – to undertake an investigation without setting out what is being investigated would be to flounder immediately. And so I begin this chapter with an exploration of some of the ways in which the silent period is constructed by language acquisition researchers, and some of the problematic aspects of those constructions, followed by an examination of the question of silence writ large in language learning.

Like its progeny *silent period*, the term *silence* seems at first blush quite unambiguous. Silence in general is simply the absence of sound; in language it is the absence of speech.[1] The silent period must therefore be a span of time where there is no talking. Can it be otherwise? Certainly for some linguists it cannot. However, for others silence is a much less clear concept. Let us examine these conflicting views.

It is apparent that a categorically silent period occurs in at least some second-language learners. Kenji Hakuta's (1976) observation of a silent period in a Japanese child learning English, and the autobiography of Richard Rodriguez (1988), in which he recounts his own silent period, are but two documented examples of the occurrence of precisely such a silence. And the anecdote told at the beginning of the introduction to this book narrates a moment at which an utterly silent period ended. Indeed, that first excited shouting, in his new language, of the young newcomer to Toronto and to English, which shattered a previously unbroken silence of several months' duration, appears initially to be an archetypal example of the concept of the silent period. For months that child did not speak at all; then he spoke suddenly, articulately, passionately, and without hesitation. Certainly such a story must fit even the most unyielding definition of silence. Paradigmatic though that example might seem, however, it would be a mistake to assume that it is entirely representative. Not all manifestations of silence in second language acquisition are as apparently unambiguous, tidy and well behaved – and it is this very messiness that invites the conflicting interpretations that inform, and arise from, linguists' attempts to understand and explain the phenomenon.

The debate concerning precisely what constitutes silence and the silent period in second language acquisition seems to coalesce around differing valuations of certain types of speech act. Specifically, some linguists draw a distinction between creative speech production on one hand, and the repetition of words and/or formulaic – essentially holophrastic – expressions on the other. They argue that a silent period is one in which the latter may occur, with varying frequency, but the former does not. Others note the distinction, but apply it differently. And still others draw no such distinction: for them, any oral language production, of any kind, ends silence, thereby nullifying the silent period. The first of these positions is articulated by Dulay *et al.* (1982), Krashen (1982, 1985) and others; the second is articulated by Saville-Troike (1988), and the third by Gibbons (1985).

In their discussion of the process of second language acquisition in children, Dulay *et al.* (1982: 22–23) initially describe the silent period as one during which learners 'concentrate on comprehension and opt for one-way or restricted two-way communication'. Later they elaborate:

    ... [C]hildren in natural host language contexts have been observed to go through a silent period of two or three months, during which they limit their speech to brief imitations and a few routines. The silent period is believed to help build up some competence through listening – enough to permit some spontaneous speech production without relying on the first language. (Dulay *et al.*, 1982: 108–109)

Neither of these observations appears to hold any suggestion that the silent period is ended by the occurrence within it of limited speech. Rather, the authors seem to recognise implicitly that 'brief imitations' and 'routines' are qualitatively different from 'spontaneous speech production'. This distinction hints at the possibility that silence in language acquisition is a more complex notion than the primary denotation of the word might indicate: not only that silence can be absolute or relative, but that a lack of absolute silence may not, in itself, signify the presence of original language production.

The same distinction, between imitative and creative language production, holds in Krashen's comparison of intra- and post-silent-period English production on the part of J. Huang's research subject Paul, a five year old whose first language was Chinese (Huang, 1970; Huang & Hatch, 1978). Paul's initial production of English was limited to sentences he had memorised, such as 'Get out of here', which he recited holophrastically; it was only later that creative language production began. Krashen (1982: 26) remarks that this later production 'looked very much like first language development, with short, simple sentences such as "This kite" ...' for 'This is a kite'. Krashen later uses his *input hypothesis* both to sum up the silent period as '[a] period of time during which the acquirer does not have enough competence to speak [and which may] vary from a few hours to several months ...' (Krashen, 1985: 103), and to explain his interpretation of the concept more thoroughly:

> The Input Hypothesis also accounts for the silent period, a phenomenon that is very noticeable in child second-language acquisition. Very typically, children in a new country, faced with a new language, are silent for a long period of time, their output being limited to a set number of memorized phrases and sentences that they hear frequently and whose meaning they do not understand completely. 'True' second-language production may not emerge for several months; a silent period of six months' duration is not unusual. (Krashen, 1985: 9)

As in Dulay *et al.* (1982), Krashen's own writing distinguishes between formulaic, rote-learned language, reproduced imitatively, and 'true' production of the second language. Here the differentiation is grounded in his hypothesis that creative language production begins only when a certain level of comprehension has been reached; during the silent period, comprehension is at best partial. Most importantly for the purpose of the present study, Krashen's understanding of the silent period is in no way inconsistent with the presence of some second language output, albeit perhaps in very limited amounts.

The distinction between imitative and creative language output is a significant one; certainly it is one that other researchers have considered. Specifically, Edith Hanania and Harry Gradman, in their work with the second language acquisition process of an adult learner, distinguish for the purpose of analysis 'between memorized utterances and constructed utterances that were created by the subject' (Hanania & Gradman, 1977: 78). While their reasons for drawing this distinction are outside the purview of my project, the fact that they make the distinction at all speaks to the legitimacy of recognising qualitative differences between imitative and creative language.

Like the researchers discussed above, Saville-Troike (1988) distinguishes between the 'repetition of others' utterances [and] recall and practice' as one kind of speech act, and the 'creation of new linguistic forms' as another. But she applies the distinction differently. For Saville-Troike, the differences between these two types of utterance, while present and noteworthy, are not the salient feature of the silent period. For her, the term *silent period* refers to a phase 'early in the course of second language development, during which [certain learners] largely cease verbal communication with speakers of the second language' (Saville-Troike 1988: 567). Her study, which categorises children as outer- or inner-directed language learners, finds that those identified as inner-directed engage in a great deal of private speech (including various strategies, among which are both imitative and creative utterances) during the silent period. She elaborates:

> Rather than being assertive in social communication, inner-directed learners by contrast typically go through a period during which they refrain from initiating interaction with speakers of the new language, and produce little if any overt social verbalization in the second language. The fact that [their] utterances ... have been found to be relatively complex when they resume communicating in the second language clearly indicates there has been no major gap in the process of their linguistic development, but that it has 'gone underground', so to speak. (Saville-Troike, 1988: 568)

Curious, but nonetheless consistent with the recognition of the silent period as idiosyncratic, is Saville-Troike's (1988) finding that the complexity of learners' utterances seems to keep apace with their exposure to the second language. It contrasts with Krashen's (1982) assertion concerning Huang's (1970) subject Paul, whose second language acquisition process following a period of silence substantially resembled that of first language acquisition. But what is also of particular interest is that although, for Saville-Troike, both imitative and creative speech acts can occur within the silent period, she does not argue against the use of the term. Instead, she amends its description: 'As defined on the basis of this study, the "silent" period is not necessarily one of categorical silence, but its onset is marked by a dramatic drop in language directed to speakers of the second language' (1988: 577).

Another interpretation of the presence within this period of imitative and repetitive speech is found in the work of John Gibbons (1985). In his examination of prevalent linguistic and curricular perspectives regarding the usefulness of the silent period, Gibbons disputes the interpretation, articulated by Dulay *et al.* (1982), of the silent period as comprising comprehension without production. He concludes, on the contrary, that any observable silence on the part of a second-language learner is probably caused by a *lack* of understanding of the target language, or by psychological rather than linguistic withdrawal (Gibbons, 1985: 261). Further, and of more immediate relevance here, Gibbons clearly expresses discomfort with the paradoxical quality of the concept of a silent period as one that can involve speech, in a way analogous to Saville-Troike in terms of observation but quite different with respect to conclusion. Gibbons appears unconvinced by the distinction that other linguists have made, with respect to the silent period, between original, creative language production and holophrastic *re*-production of memorised utterances; indeed he is troubled by it. 'To regard routines and patterns as silence', he writes, 'is somewhat disconcerting' (Gibbons, 1985: 257). While both of Gibbons' propositions have relevance here, for the moment my response to his work engages his position on what he seems to argue is a paradox: speech occurring within the so-called silent period.

Notwithstanding the debates surrounding the issue of how silence is to be defined, there are methodological difficulties inherent in the study of silence that translate into logistical problems in the field. I refer in particular to Hakuta's (1976) case study of a Japanese-speaking child learning English, and to Gibbons' discussion of that study. Gibbons dismisses the Hakuta study as failing to offer evidence for a silent period. Arguing that 'Hakuta's study ... began three months after [the child] entered kindergarten, so she was already speaking English when the study began', Gibbons (1985: 256) finds it puzzling that the work is referred to as often as it is.

But Hakuta himself notes, with respect to his subject's silent period, that 'prior to the first sample, in fact from three months after her exposure to English began, I made repeated attempts to gather data, but she produced little speech' (Hakuta, 1976: 322). It seems, then, that the child in Hakuta's study did, in fact, undergo a silent period – at least as would be defined by Krashen – and that the researcher, who 'chose to let her begin speaking in a natural environment', simply found no usefulness in investigating her silence. This perceived lack of utility is interesting on its own, inasmuch as it exemplifies the tendency in research to overlook silence, by dint of the common-sense perception of it as an empty phenomenon rather than as an object of study. But of concern in the present context, with regard to Gibbons' disagreement with the concept of the silent period, is the fact that the study began when the subject's silence was coming to an end; this fact is evidence for, rather than against, a silent period.

Further, Gibbons does recognise the Huang (1970) study, although he argues that the discrepancy in duration of the silent periods of that study's subject may have been caused by distinct environmental influences or personality differences. Still, to argue for either of these possibilities is to acknowledge implicitly the presence of a period of silence. Clearly, while it is axiomatic to say that incomprehension must certainly be what informs that silence at the beginning of the second language acquisition process, it is worth remembering Saville-Troike's observation, noted above, that the complexity of learners' utterances 'when they resume communicating in the second language clearly indicates there has been no major gap in the process of their linguistic development' (Saville-Troike, 1988: 568). It seems somewhat counter-intuitive to suggest, as Gibbons appears to do, that a silent period, if one does exist, is a time of utter incomprehension followed by an instantaneous onset (presumably at the moment of the first creative utterance) of full comprehension and competent production.

To state that Gibbons equates creative and imitative language production would be to oversimplify his position, especially given that he argues for the value of 'routines and patterns as a facilitator of social interaction when productive rules have not yet been acquired' (Gibbons, 1985: 257), thereby ordering imitative and creative language production hierarchically with respect to complexity. Still, he does seem to be saying that where there is talk there cannot be silence. Of course, on one level this statement is patently true; for me, however, the reasoning informing the statement warrants scrutiny. On the face of it, the idea of a silent period that may not actually be silent *is* tricky, even uncomfortable. Initially I, like Gibbons, experience discomfort in labelling as silent a stage in which there is in fact sound. It seems that, if language is being produced, however rudimentary that language might be, the stage of production can hardly be called silent. But my concern here is with the quality of the silence (and relatedly, with the quality of the speech), rather than the simple fact of it. The silence that concerns me, and which subsequent chapters will both affirm and explore, is the silence, whether its imposition is conscious or unconscious, of the self. I therefore find compelling and helpful the distinction drawn by Krashen and Saville-Troike between language that expresses creatively and language that merely repeats.

It has become axiomatic to say that in language acquisition, whether first or second, comprehension precedes production. This view is consistent with Gibbons' (1985) position that it is a lack of comprehension that prevents speech at the very beginning of second language acquisition. His observation that children 'placed in a school where they do not speak the local language are surrounded ... by a miasma of incomprehensible speech ... [and] might take some time to sort and make sense of the flood of input' (Gibbons, 1985: 261) is quite indisputable. Nor, incidentally, is it disputed by, or contradictory to, the claims of Dulay *et al.* and others (for example, Hakuta, 1976; Eric Lenneberg, 1962). But it does seem counter-intuitive to suggest that creative, speaker-generated speech production can be equated, for the sake of determining what is or is not acquired language, with the imitation of rote phrases. The former type of utterance demands, at a minimum, syntactic or semantic comprehension, albeit perhaps at a very basic level, while the latter – consisting of imitation and repetition – requires only the ability to recall and reproduce phonological features. A couple of simple examples corroborate this view: the ability to put to good use the mimicry of 'foreign' expressions that have been heard but that are not understood is a common experience for the traveller; and even parrots can be trained to repeat short sentences. It hardly needs to be pointed out that this level of production is qualitatively different from creative language production.

Despite Gibbons' reluctance to acknowledge wholeheartedly the claims made by other linguists regarding a silent period in second language acquisition, he does propose, in the conclusion to his examination of it, that curricula recognise a period of 'reduced output' on the part of the learner at the beginning of the second language acquisition process (Gibbons, 1985: 265). I suggest that one of the features of such a 'reduced output' period is that whatever output may be present tends not to be original, except perhaps by accident; for the most part it consists of imitative repetition of words and phrases learned by rote. It should not, therefore, be looked on as constituting authentic, original language production. I further suggest that this lack of original output can be understood as silence *vis-à-vis* authentic, original, creative production of speech in the second language. It is this argument that informs the concept of the silent period as I interpret it for the purpose of this study: as one kind of silence.

And yet to have reached the determination that what counts as authentically acquired second language is original, creative speech production is to have barely begun. What I put forward as a possible next step in approaching the admittedly (and I contend necessarily) nebulous concept of the silent period is to consider it as part of the answer to a larger question: *what are second-language learners doing in addition to learning a second language*? More precisely, what are they doing with, and in, that second language, when they are silent with respect to some – or all – aspects of its production? For the learner of a second language is implicated in another, and to me a more profound, kind of silence. I refer here to a silence not just of the vocal apparatus but of the *self*: a silence, that is, which may be symptomatic of a kind of suspension between two linguistic selves, occurring in a kind of moment that is both linguistic and psychical within the complex process (itself not merely linguistic, but also psychical) of moving from one language to another and, simultaneously, from one linguistic self to another. For me, this is the significant and underlying silence of which the observed, and much debated, silent period may be a symptom. And studying this silence is no simple undertaking.

But examining the arguably more obvious silent period is not an easy task either, for what I am now faced with is the study of something that by my own definition is, in a very important sense, absent. Dictionaries define silence primarily with words such as *absence* (of sound or noise), *inability* (to speak) and *omission* (of mention),[2] while secondary definitions, such as 'abstinence from, or renunciation of, speech' or in other cases 'a period of time without speech or noise' and 'refusal or failure to speak out'[3] are likewise shadowed with connotations that imply a lack, an absence, an emptiness: something that is not, rather than something that is.

This is to be expected. Western positivist tradition takes an interest in what can be seen and heard: what cannot be seen or heard is often not attended to at all, much less described or explained. Moreover, even what *can* be seen and heard is often difficult, and sometimes impossible, to understand, not least because of what seems to be missing, or absent, or left out – and which, because it is left out, cannot even be identified.

So the task before me is a complex one. For, however I approach it, however I define it, silence is, after all, silent. It will not give up its story easily. And while for these reasons it would be difficult to work with silence in any context, to attempt to examine the silent period as a stage within the second language learning process I must try to tease apart a doubly complex problem. The study of how a second language is acquired may arguably be regarded very generally as primarily occupying itself with the process of production. It deals with what is produced, and when, and how, and how quickly, in regard to the aspects and patterns that it interprets as universal and, by extension, with variations to that universality. Ellis's overview of the history of SLA research articulates this focus as embodying a search for 'universal properties of L2 acquisition – looking for commonalities across learners of different ages, in different settings and with different L1s' (Ellis, 1996: 2). And this is understandable – why should it be otherwise? As I have noted above, thinking about language, and consequently language research, seems to mean thinking about speaking, and listening, and understanding. These are active processes; silence in relation to language is intuitively understood as the absence of these active processes.

Metaphors of common usage render silence as an empty container, waiting to be filled. Even when silence is 'golden' it is its emptiness, its stillness, that makes it so. But writers and poets, who work in words, know that silence expresses much that speech cannot: the metaphorical emptiness of silence is betrayed by literature and poetry, which voice other intuitions, different metaphors. In searching for ways to make language 'justly convey the shape and vitality' of those 'actions of the spirit rooted in silence' that George Steiner (1970: 12) refers to, it may be instructive to look to literary genres for ways of broadening and deepening our thinking about language that allow it to encompass that silence which lies in the spaces between the words. Aldous Huxley (1978), in *Point Counter Point*, portrays silence as solid and rich with possibility, 'as full of potential wisdom and wit as the unhewn marble of great sculpture'. And for Thomas Carlyle (1970), 'Under all speech that is good for anything there lies a silence that is better. Silence is deep as Eternity; speech is shallow as Time'. Silence as an object of study is elusive, to be sure, but elusiveness is an insufficient argument for the exclusion of such an important aspect from the study of a process as complex as the acquisition of a language. And difficult though it may be to move from the 'common-sense' belief of silence as an absence to its acknowledgement as a presence, and subsequently to an attempt to investigate it, it is a move worth making.

## Individual Differences

Placing aside for the moment the question of silence as a psychical phenomenon, and keeping to the level of the silent period as observed by linguistic research, it is apparent, from the preceding discussion concerning what constitutes silence in second language learning, that research in this field is no stranger to elusiveness or to ambiguity. An examination of the work of Brown (1994a), Larsen-Freeman and Long (1991), Lightbown and Spada (1996), and Skehan (1989), which organises itself under the over-arching classification known as *individual differences*, reveals a striking lack of consensus on numerous key research issues. And although there seems to be a substantial degree of commonality between one schema and the next, researchers vary in their descriptions and categorisations of precisely which factors influence such differences.

Ellis describes individual differences as, generally, 'the differences in how learners learn an L2, how fast they learn, and how successful they are ... [including] both general factors such as language learning aptitude and motivation, and specific learner strategies' (Ellis, 1996: 707). Peter Skehan (1989: 110–115) cites extroversion, introversion and anxiety as individual differences. H. Douglas Brown (1994a: 163) refers to three mutually informing categories: the first he names *styles and strategies*: which comprise, among others, learning and reasoning styles, left- and right-brain functioning and the tolerance of ambiguity (Brown, 1994a: 103). Second, he cites *sociocultural factors*:

> an aspect that is still very much a part of the egocentric self in a transactional process but a specialized subset of that process: ... the over-coming of the personal and transactional barriers presented by two cultures in contact, and the relationship of culture learning to language learning. (Brown, 1994a: 163)

The third factor Brown calls *personality*, including in it self-esteem, affect, anxiety, extroversion and motivation (Brown, 1994a: 134). Similarly, Lightbown and Spada (1996: 33–34) claim a model of second language acquisition that encompasses individual learner characteristics such as intelligence, aptitude and learning styles, personality, motivation and atti-tudes, and age of acquisition.

Larsen-Freeman and Long (1991) take a similar approach. First, they name the following principal determinants of what they term *differential success*: language aptitude, social-psychological factors, personality, cogni-tive style, age, hemisphere specialisation, learning strategies and other factors, including memory and sex (Larsen-Freeman & Long, 1991: 153). It appears that with a little overlap the first four of their categories substan-tially parallel Brown's three categories, while the remaining three isolate factors that could arguably fall within Brown's somewhat broader catego-ries. Urged forward by Larry Selinker's proposition which holds that 'a theory of second language learning that does not provide a central place for individual differences among learners *cannot* be considered acceptable'

(Selinker, 1972: 213, fn 8), Larsen-Freeman and Long (1991) undertake a detailed discussion of the factors they name as significant and provide a helpful overview of the ways in which SLA research has dealt with them. They delve past that first layer of recognition to consider possible reasons why those factors affect the second language acquisition process the way(s) they do, and in so doing note that often there is no full consensus about whether a given variable affects that process at all. Nor, if it is deemed significant, is there consensus as to its actual influences.

Despite their acknowledgement of this lack of consensus, Larsen-Freeman and Long (1991: 173) nevertheless advance various explanations for such differences. And in so doing they occasionally allude to questions of identity that approach those on which my own inquiry focuses. In their examination of motivation, for example, they acknowledge the contributions of Donald Mowrer (1950), specifically his ideas concerning the relationship between the search for identification and successful language acquisition. In particular, they connect his idea to the phenomenon that Robert Gardner and Wallace Lambert (1972) subsequently named *integrative motivation*. In addition, Larsen-Freeman and Long (1991: 181) discuss the substantial, yet substantially inconclusive, body of work on attitudes among second-language learners, especially with reference to the attitudes of those students towards each other, their teachers and the language they are learning. They acknowledge SLA theories, among them Gardner's (1985) 'socio-educational model', that 'embrace constellations of [social-psychological factors] and indeed perceive [them] as being central to an understanding of SLA ...'. Larsen-Freeman and Long further affirm the view, based in part on Gardner's work, that:

> one's identity is very much bound up with the language one speaks, [and that] the process of acquiring a second language forces a re-evaluation of one's self-image and the successful integration of new social and cultural ideas. (Larsen-Freeman & Long, 1991: 181)

Their discussion of the categorical framework of 'personality' likewise includes aspects that might be considered to fall generally within the domain of *attitudes* and which, to the extent that they do so, seem to be related to ideas about identity as understood by these researchers – more precisely, attitudes held by language learners towards themselves and their abilities, such as self-esteem, and attitudes (on the part of both teachers and learners) towards learner characteristics such as extroversion and introversion. Within that same category Larsen-Freeman and Long also include anxiety, risk-taking, sensitivity to rejection, inhibition and tolerance of ambiguity – learner characteristics that have been studied extensively.

Larsen-Freeman and Long's review of the research in these areas is comprehensive, but it leaves me both curious and troubled. Their discussion conveys the sense of significant consensus among SLA researchers as to the factors that influence the pattern of an individual's second language acquisition. And it is initially easy to find comfort in that consensus. But an attempt to examine precisely how these factors work results in the fabric of both the consensus and the comfort beginning to fray.

Let us briefly consider anxiety. Krashen's *affective filter hypothesis* (1985: 3) states that 'when the acquirer is unmotivated, lacking in self-confidence, or anxious' she or he may not be able to employ fully the 'comprehensible input [that] is necessary for acquisition', and that 'while we have made some real progress in describing the general characteristics of the affective filter ... there is considerable individual variation' (Krashen, 1985: 44). The view of anxiety as one of the individual differences that affect success or failure in second language learning is supported by a considerable amount of research (including Brown, 1994a; Larsen-Freeman & Long, 1991; and Lightbown & Spada, 1996). But the results of these studies have varied substantially. Referring to an earlier review of learner anxiety studies (MacIntyre & Gardner, 1991), Ellis (1996) notes that '... not all the studies in [that] review produced significant correlations between anxiety and achievement'. Similarly, he draws on other earlier work (Ely, 1986; Parkinson & Howell-Richardson, 1990; and Young, 1986) to assert that '... studies of learner anxiety have often produced even more mixed results' (Ellis, 1996: 482).

It is undoubtedly the case that anxiety is a phenomenon intrinsically difficult to describe and to measure. But it is also my contention that the efforts of SLA research to distinguish between and study several types of anxiety, while admirable, fall peculiarly short of the mark even as, ironically, they point directly towards it. Ellis (1996: 479), for example, outlines the distinction drawn in the literature between 'trait anxiety, state anxiety, and situation-specific anxiety'. He cites Thomas Scovel's (1978) definition of trait anxiety as 'a "more permanent disposition to be anxious" ... perhaps best viewed as an aspect of personality' (Ellis, 1996: 479) in support of his later assertion that 'learners can also experience anxiety as a result of fear or experience of "losing oneself in the target culture"' and that they may experience, as manifestations of anxiety, 'emotional regression, panic, anger, self-pity, indecision, sadness, alienation' (Oxford, 1992; cited in Ellis, 1996: 480).

Somewhat relatedly, in a 1980 paper Peter Harder points to silence as a response to gaps that may exist in an second-language learner's communicative potential, based on the linguistic conventions (which Harder calls *system*) accessible to that learner as well as on the invocation, or *actualisation*, of whichever of those accessible conventions might be useful at a given moment (Harder, 1980: 263). For Harder the latter is at the mercy of the former: insufficient access to linguistic conventions can mean that the learner

> is not free to define his place in the ongoing interaction ... [but rather] ... has to accept a role which is less desirable than he could ordinarily achieve ... [since] ... free choice of action depends on free choice of convention. (Harder, 1980: 267–268)

One of the implications for the learner experiencing anxiety as a result of this reduced role is a dilemma that silence might address:

> Most learners will probably, in deciding what to say (if anything) have a sort of cut-off point for the reduction they will tolerate, below which silence is preferable. Instead of seeing silence as the extreme point on the scale of message reduction, it can also be seen as the alternative to it. (Harder, 1980: 169)

Harder further speculates that, if the issue giving rise to the dilemma of whether to speak or to remain silent is not clearly addressed (a dilemma he summarises, succinctly and with humour, as the requirement that 'in order to be a wit in a foreign language... [a language learner must]..go through the stage of being a half-wit'), 'learners may just be aware of it as a constant internal resistance against opening their mouths' (Harder, 1980: 269).

All of this language – losing the self, anger, indecision, alienation, tolerability, internal resistance – seems to intimate the need for engagement with a discourse that regards anxiety as a deeply existential concern rather than, or in addition to, a personality trait. Yet SLA research seems to hold back from such an engagement, remaining, in effect, silent on the concept of silence. In my own desire to converse with that silence, I will turn, in the next chapter, to a consideration of how anxiety might be seen through the lens of psychoanalytic theory. But for now it is important to note that the literature abounds, as Larsen-Freeman and Long (1991) point out, with inconclusive statements concerning research into various factors – not just anxiety – that are believed to result in differences between individuals' acquisition of a second language. This fact, of few conclusive findings despite the consensus, is the second conspicuous feature that this overview of SLA research reveals. Larsen-Freeman and Long certainly recognise it, not without irony. In their words:

> We are well aware that our readers, particularly those who *are more intolerant of ambiguity*, might feel frustrated in reading this chapter in

which few answers are furnished to questions about differential success among second-language learners. It is certainly true that many of the studies reviewed here yield inconclusive or contradictory findings. Practical implications must therefore remain tenuous at best. (Larsen-Freeman & Long, 1991: 206; my italics)

While Larsen-Freeman and Long (1991: 206) do go on to state that 'some of the research findings reported [in their book] have been interpreted as supporting a particular educational practice', their recognition of the general inconclusiveness of the research is telling. Clearly, second language acquisition is a very complex process, the investigation of which requires, as they point out, an ability to tolerate a multiplicity of contributing factors, divergent evidence and unpredictable, often surprising, conclusions. After all, any specific factor may be either a cause or an effect of either success or failure in second language acquisition. For example, high self-esteem might allow for less difficulty in language learning, but it might also be a result of previous success. Similarly, a negative attitude on the part of a learner might result in success if the individual's goal is to dominate the language and thereby its speakers; the same attitude might result in a failure if the learner has no desire to identify or communicate with speakers of the target language.

With respect to age as an indicator of second language acquisition success, Ellis (1996) remarks that it too is far from transparent; while some studies indicate that 'younger is better and, therefore, [offer] some support for the Critical Period Hypothesis', Ellis (1996: 489) notes that other work, by Birgit Harley (1986), has demonstrated more rapid learning and greater achievement by older students. Granted, these studies have not tested for identical variables, and therefore ought not to be expected to produce identical results, but what is clearly the case is that, despite the obvious ease (relative to other factors such as personality and motivation) of measuring age, 'the relationship between a learner's age and his or her potential for success in second language acquisition is the subject of much lively debate' (Lightbown & Spada, 1996: 41).

There is no shortage of writing like this. The debate may be lively, but it is also, frustratingly yet unavoidably, full of the ambivalence and ambiguity characteristic of much human undertaking. What it is *not* is either surprising or exhaustive. In the story of the young boy recognising the snake at the zoo, related in the introduction, the child's speaking arose at the right moment, out of his silence: that he did not speak before did not mean he had nothing to say. Similarly, the lack of conclusive answers in many areas of SLA research is certainly no indication that there is nothing to be known.

## From Personality to Identity

Indeed, it is this lack of answers that leads me to consider the possibility that perhaps there is also a sense in which the questions may be inadequate. I have discussed two striking features of the SLA research into individual differences: first, the relative consensus about what those features are, and second, the widely divergent ideas about precisely how they act upon the language acquisition process. For me, a third significant feature of the work reviewed by Larsen-Freeman and Long (1991) – as also of Ehrman and Dörnyei's (1998) text on inter- and intra-personal dynamics in second language education – and the point at which this literature becomes compelling for my own project, is its recurrent mention of identity and concepts related to it, such as the self-esteem and attitudes discussed above. Even so, although the literature mentions these concepts, and in some cases even works quite intensively with some aspects of them, it nevertheless seems to me that, oddly, something might be missing from the way in which SLA research conceptualises identity.

Or perhaps it is not so odd; SLA research was born of the science of linguistics, nurtured by a psycholinguistic approach primarily concerned with cognition, and more recently step-parented by sociolinguistic perspectives (Ellis, 1996: 1). Initially occupying itself with the characteristics and properties of learner language, it has moved towards including an examination of issues of affect, but in a sense it seems uncertain about how to proceed. And no wonder – the problem of the identity of the subject is both immeasurably problematic to perceive and perceptibly difficult to measure and analyse. And when we combine the problems of identity, perception, measurement and analysis with the idea of studying, not language as such, but rather silence *within* language, the difficulty becomes more daunting still. What exactly is lacking, and what can be done about it?

This discussion is by no means intended to imply that SLA research has failed to notice silence; important examinations of the silent period, for example, have been made, and some of them are outlined above. Very generally, in the linguistics literature there seem to be three principal frameworks for explaining silence in second language learning. As already discussed, there are the two contrasting contentions that silence is either the result of a concentration on comprehension during the early stages of acquisition (Dulay *et al.*, 1982) or the manifestation of a lack of comprehension of the target language during that period (Gibbons, 1985). While these theories seem to contradict each other somewhat, in effect they are two sides of the same coin – both are underpinned by a supposition that speech production (or lack of it) is predicated directly upon comprehension.

A third view is intimated in Harder's speculation that silence is the consequence of a 'constant internal resistance against opening [one's] mouth' – a resistance of which the individual learner him- or herself 'may just be aware' (Harder, 1980: 269). This conceptualisation of silence as arising out of difficulties related to performance (specifically, concern about one's performance as reduced or otherwise inadequate) is not entirely unrelated to the comprehension/lack-of-comprehension views elucidated by Dulay *et al.* (1982) and Gibbons (1985), since there is clearly a significant interrelationship between comprehension and production. It is, however, my contention that this relationship might be more complicated than these two assessments suggest.

While Harder, for example, in postulating silence as internally generated, invites consideration of the possibility that something other than consciousness might be implicated in the manifestation of silence, his invitation nevertheless seems almost inadvertent. It is certainly peripheral to his central argument, which is that silence is the result of a learner's dilemma (concerning whether, in a given situation, to assume a reduced role in communication or decline to communicate at all) that can be overcome if learners 'are told that this is *not* just their individual dilemma' (Harder, 1980: 269; my italics).

This view, and the contradictory yet related comprehension/lack-of-comprehension views elucidated by Dulay *et al.* (1982) and Gibbons (1985) respectively, are surely significant for their recognition of silence as an indication of something more than a mere absence of speech. For me, however, they seem to simplify rather than satisfy. Where they remain wanting is in the gap they leave between the fact of silence (whether defined as a silent period, or more generally) and an enquiry into the relationship between that silence and the subjective experience of the individual engaged in second language acquisition. That such a gap should persist seems somehow odd, since within SLA research there is no lack of discussion of subjective and idiosyncratic elements that may contribute to, detract from, and in general interact with the process of an individual's second language learning. Much of the discussion of individual personality factors effectively knocks at the door of the questions concerning identity that I wish to engage, but disappoints in its failure to go through that door and look at what is on the other side. Might we perhaps consider silence as more than just a direct and exclusively linguistic consequence of either a concentration on – or a lack of – comprehension, as Dulay *et al.* (1982) and Gibbons (1985) would have it? Equally, might silence originate in or be a symptom of something other than, or additional to, the problem of incomplete access to the conventions of the target language, as Harder (1980) seems to suggest?

That is, might there be something at stake, more or other than the reduction of a linguistic role per se, in the process of second language acquisition?

Saville-Troike's (1988) discussion about the lack of interest in private speech within first language acquisition research resonates with my own belief that SLA research is, likewise, insufficiently curious about silence as a part of the second language learning process. Following the view of George Miller, articulated in his introduction to Ruth Weir's *Language in the Crib* (Weir, 1970: 15), Saville-Troike writes that:

> the dominant conception of language learning as critically involving responses to the stimuli and reinforcements of a supportive environment had led to a focus on mother–child dyadic interaction, and entailed the assumption that nothing 'interesting' was taking place when a child was alone, and in the dark. (Saville-Troike, 1988: 568)

Saville-Troike proceeds to extend this judgement to SLA research. Her reasoning bears quoting at some length:

> While strictly behaviourist theories are no longer in vogue, the now-dominant conception of language learning as critically involving social/interpersonal interaction has left potentially important ... non-interactive phenomena generally out of researchers' awareness. Further, there has been a tendency in the second language learning field to equate overt production with active learning, and lack of overt production with passivity and disengagement. These conceptual perspectives ... have led to an unconscious assumption that nothing of significance was happening unless learners were talking to others. (Saville-Troike, 1988: 568–69)

As I have indicated, it is my view that 'something of significance' is indeed happening, even when learners are silent. And, despite the perception of silence as empty that appears to prevail within SLA research, and which Saville-Troike calls an *unconscious assumption*, some linguists do allude to the possibility of a relationship between language learning and the identity of the individual in addition to, or apart from, that individual's linguistic interactions with others. Guiora *et al.* (1972: 111–12) put forward the idea that 'the task of learning a second language poses a challenge to the integrity of basic identifications ... [and involves] extending the self so as to take on a new identity', and Leslie Beebe (1983: 40), in a discussion of risk-taking in language learning, contends that learners may 'fear a loss of identity'. Brown (1994a: 62), in his outline of affective considerations, hints at the role of what he calls self-identity in language acquisition. Brown suggests that younger (and therefore more egocentric and less self-conscious) children may learn languages more easily because their identities are less formed, and he puts forward the idea that adults learning a second language, by contrast, must overcome inhibitions in order to make 'the leap into a new or second identity'. And similarly, even Gibbons, whose claims initially seem effectively to dismiss the notion of a silent period altogether and who overtly retains a very guarded view of silence, ultimately implicitly both accepts its actuality and acknowledges its idiosyncratic qualities by proposing that 'if silence persists beyond a few weeks, then individual psychological factors can probably provide an explanation' (Gibbons, 1985: 261).

Clearly, then, linguists are not unaware of the possibility that unconscious factors and questions of identity might have a role to play in the aspect of silence in second language acquisition. But their awareness does not seem to go quite far enough. My reading of their commentaries leaves me with the impression that what is taking place is a kind of not-quite-speaking, a thought brought momentarily to consciousness and then dismissed, an approach made towards engagement with the question of identity, but followed quickly by a retreat: a retreat, it would seem, into a place of silence *about* silence.

Yes, something seems to be missing from SLA research's disquisition on silence. Whether it has been forgotten, or neglected, or misplaced, or was never quite found at all, just now it seems to be positioned somewhere outside the field of perception. It is as if a kind of collective unconscious is at work, an aspect of SLA research that in a sense is not even aware of itself and that is consequently unable to address itself. I suggest that where SLA research is left wanting is in its failure to account adequately for, and to effectively consider, something that I believe is crucial to the assessment of individual differences in language acquisition. That is, while SLA research locates and names individual differences, and even at times broaches the question of identity as it relates to those differences, its analysis, I contend, seems to neglect components of identity, or self, or self-concept, which to me are of even greater significance, and which operate within the individual at a still deeper, intra-personal level to inform those differences. This element is, simply put, the identity, or self, or self-concept, of the individual subject.

## From the Individual to the Social ...

Still, if SLA research does not quite know its own silences, it nevertheless hints at the possibility of knowing them. My search is for a discourse that complements and extends that more positivist SLA literature, that takes up those hints. In anticipation of thinking specifically about the acquisition of a second language and its relation to the making and remaking of the self, it is helpful to consider the process of identity formation, particularly as it is interwoven with language writ large. The importance of language as a means for making relations between the world and the self (and, as I will argue later, between different aspects of the self) is addressed in various areas of the social sciences. And these social theories offer some hints of their own that might be instructive for thinking about individuals' identities, and the work of making those identities, as it is performed in the world and through language.

Rom Harré's work on the importance of discourse in the field of social constructionism begins with a disclaimer (Harré, 1993: 3). While not disputing the concept of individual humans as 'artefacts, products of social process', the most important of which are linguistic and otherwise discursive, Harré refuses the assumption that individual action is always and only socially caused. Individuals, according to Harré, 'are built to be capable of autonomous action'. Significantly for this study, that autonomous action includes the social construction of meaning; for Harré 'the meanings of social events are created, not given' (Harré, 1993: 77). Although it is in social contexts that this creative meaning-making takes place, it is individuals who do the creating, and it is through the symbols of language that they do it. Moreover, the symbols could not exist without these individuals – 'there could not be languages and discursive processes unless there were brains buzzing ... and vibrations in the air and marks on paper' (Harré & Gillett, 1994: 100), just as there could be no social contexts, no 'pattern[s] or array[s] of institutions and material and discursive practices' (Harré, 1993: 204) without the participation of individuals in them.

Standing in partial contrast to Harré is Ian Burkitt (1991), who presents a critique of traditional views that maintain that the individual's self and the world are separate entities in opposition to each other. In Burkitt's conception of the self as social, and of human beings as continually engaged in social relations, there is little space for a view, such as Harré's, of the self as autonomous, as capable of acting on the world as well as interacting with it. Burkitt charges Harré with arguing contradictory claims: on one hand, that 'the public and collective order [is] the basis for social and personal being', and on the other hand that 'the social order is ... created by the intentional actions of individuals' (Burkitt, 1991: 75).

While he does not suggest that the notion of the individual is altogether false, Burkitt does privilege the claim that individuality is socially based, and that common-sense Western understandings of the individual human being as a 'psychological monad' (Burkitt, 1991: 17), whose individuality is established at birth, are erroneous. He further rejects the notion of meaning-making as a function of the individual mind as, at best, incomplete (1991: 84–85), since for him such interpretations fail to take sufficient account of society itself as a creator of meaning. Rather, he holds that personality is created by forces external to the individual, and shaped by power relations, whose 'repression [takes] the initiatives and motives for action away from rational control' (1991: 214).

With regard to the question of language as one of these social forces, Burkitt (1991) draws heavily on the George Mead's contention (1934) that the means by which we individuals come to know our own experiences is through knowing others' experiences of us, specifically by becoming 'objects to ourselves' – absorbing and adopting others' perceptions of ourselves 'within a social environment or context of experience and behaviour in which both [we] and they are involved' (Mead, 1934: 138). For Mead, and for Burkitt, it is language – 'communication in the sense of significant symbols ... directed not only to others but also to the individual himself' (Mead, 1934: 139) – that permits this process of self-objectification. Burkitt's view of individuality, or the self, as something that develops rather than being present from birth, similarly echoes Mead's contention that 'the self ... arises in the process of social experience and activity, that is, develops in the given individual as a result of his relations to that process as a whole and to other individuals within that process' (Mead, 1934: 199). Neither Mead nor Burkitt orders subjectivity prior to sociality. On the contrary, they conceptualise communicative acts as forming, and informing, 'the capacity for subjective reflection' that becomes self-consciousness (Burkitt, 1991: 34–35). Similarly, Harré's (1993: 4) view of the self as a mutable, socially informed 'location, not a substance or an attribute' that comes into being in contexts in which an individual is 'already treated as [a person] by the others of their family and tribe', is reminiscent of Mead's construction of the self-as-object-to-itself.

Discussion concerning the relationship between language, thought and identity has also located itself in sociolinguistics since the time of the Sapir-Whorf hypothesis. Edward Sapir's (1929: 162) contention that 'the "real world" is to a large extent unconsciously built up on the language habits of the group' foreshadowed Benjamin Whorf's statement, nearly three decades later, that '... the world is presented in a kaleidoscopic flux of impressions that have to be organised ... largely by the linguistic systems in our minds' (Whorf, 1956: 213). These assertions, like those of Mead (1934) and Harré (1993) relating to the social self modelling for the individual self, harmonise with Lev Vygotsky's understanding of 'the true direction of the development of thinking [as moving] not from the individual to the social, but from the social to the individual' (Vygotsky, 1997: 36). Indeed, according to William Frawley and James Lantolf, Vygotsky maintained that 'a human being is from the outset social (i.e. dialogical) and then develops into an individual (i.e. monological) entity' (Frawley & Lantolf, 1984: 146). And Lacanian thought, arguably, goes even further with respect to the relationship between language and the self. Lacan's argument, asserts Bruce Fink, is that 'without language there would be no desire as we know it – exhilarating, and yet contorted, contradictory, and loath to be satisfied – nor would there be any subject as such' (Fink, 1996: 76).

## ... And Back, from the Social to the Individual

A great deal of controversy has succeeded the linguistic determinism of the Sapir–Whorf hypothesis; in its strongest form it has largely been found inadequate. Still, the view currently privileged in sociolinguistics, and paralleled in the social theories outlined above, is rooted substantially in the concept of a mutually-informing relationship between the individual, language and culture. In other words, language and culture function, together with the material individual, to form a social subject, whose self-hood is not unitary but is constantly being created and re-created in negoti-ation with the social world outside itself. Philip Riley (1991) clearly sets out this relationship in his paper on the development of identity in the bilin-gual child. He asserts that social identity is defined through culture, culture is based on social knowledge, and social knowledge is acquired, through the medium of language, in negotiation between individuals and groups (Riley, 1991: 275). Jay Lemke (1995) is also worth quoting here, at some length, for his contention that not only our sense of self as such, but also our very sense of having a self at all, depend on interaction between the 'inside' and the 'outside':

Our *personal identity* is constructed by foregrounding certain patterns that we make in our inner dialogue and feelings as we set them against the background of what we are taught to take as 'outer' events. Needless to say, what is 'inner' and what is 'outer', what the repertory of human emotions is taken to be ... and the nature of 'inner dialogues' as activity structures, all differ from culture to culture and from one sub-community and social group (age group, gender category, social class, etc.), even from one biographical individual to another. We can take this analysis one final critical step further. We can ask how our very sense of selfhood, the notion that we *are* perceiving, experiencing, willing, acting egos, that we are/have 'minds', feelings, perceptions, desires, memo-ries, etc. is itself a construction woven from the warp and woof of cultural semiotics, such as language, categories, values, practices, in accordance with the learned patterns of our community. (Lemke, 1995: 89; italics in original)

Despite their differences, then, the social theorists' views to which I have referred embody some striking similarities. Moreover, in the context of my own examination of second language acquisition, these views can be interpreted as having more in common with aspects of psychoanalytic theory than might at first glance be perceived. I will turn to that discussion shortly. For the moment, it is instructive to expand a little on the central claim that they share, even though the lenses through which they regard it are differently coloured. That overarching idea is that, regardless of originary directionality (i.e. whether the social gives rise to the individual or the inverse) the two are interwoven, bound together in a mutually-informing relation, and moreover that language is an important – arguably the single most important – thread joining them.

As mentioned above, Vygotskyan theory holds that the individual develops from a social being that is not unique, and that only after this development into uniqueness has taken place can individuals join in dialogic relationship with others (Frawley & Lantolf, 1984: 146). This contention, along with the central claim of the social theorists named earlier that the individual and the social are interconnected, is concisely summed up by Claude Lévi-Strauss, in his work on Marcel Mauss, as a 'complementarity of individual psychical structure and social structure' (Lévi-Strauss, 1987: 22). From this premise (that the individual self is created, and continuously re-created, in a context of historical and contemporary social relationships) it is but a short intellectual step to the insight that language, both as a primary means by which the social 'outside' represents and communicates itself to the 'inside' self, and conversely as a means of expression of that self to the 'outside', is likewise grounded in and crucial to social relationships. Thus, while the particular discovery of language and its functions is clearly no small task, it is also the case that young children have a great deal more than language to discover.

Seen from this perspective, a period of silence before the acquisition of the first language might be understood as a moment considerably more complex and multi-layered than is suggested by Ellis, who claims that the silent period exists merely because 'the young child needs to discover what language is and what it does' (Ellis, 1996: 82). For it is accurate to say, using the same descriptive framework, that children have also to discover what their world, their culture, is and does, and what they themselves are, and do, and can do. And this process is not a passive one. In the sense that language acquisition includes the creative use of language and that, in turn, language is creatively used in the ongoing making and remaking of the self, the discovery of one's world and the creation of one's self (however they might be mutually informing) are similarly creative activities. These complex personal processes – the finding, or making, of a world, and the construction of a self – both include the discovery of language and are, in turn, facilitated and mediated by that language once discovered.

Like the important and complex discoveries outlined above, the acquisition of a first language is a complicated process. In addition to the physical development that is required in order to make the vocal apparatus functional, there is an enormous amount of discovering, and learning, and creating that a young child has to do, only part of which (albeit an extremely important part) is acquiring the specific forms and structures of a particular language. Consequently, it is not difficult to make a case for a period of silence with respect to first language production, nor to regard that silent period as one in which the knowledge obtained from the social world results in some originary, pre-linguistic self-concept that can then go on to be transformed, expressed and communicated through language. But what about the process of acquiring a second language?

A great deal has been written about many of the complexities inherent in second language acquisition. On the one hand, there are the structural and functional complications of the new language itself, and the complex relations between it and the first language. On the other hand, as noted earlier in this chapter and in the Introduction, there are the myriad metalinguistic and paralinguistic practices and cultural expectations that must be learned, particularly in the case of the 'foreigner' suddenly immersed in a new environment, in order for a high level of second language proficiency to be achieved. In *Many Voices* (1983), Jane Miller's work on bilingualism, she quotes from Alfred Schutz's (1964) essay, entitled 'The stranger', which speaks eloquently of the immigrant as an 'outsider' who lacks the 'logic of everyday thinking ... [and] ... trustworthy recipes for interpreting the social world ...' and who 'approaches the other group as a newcomer in the true meaning of the term' (Schutz, 1964: 95). Miller continues:

> Schutz includes language within this picture ... and in distinguishing between the passive understanding of a language and its active mastering as a means for realising one's own acts and thoughts makes language an analogue for culture ... Learned with a first language, and by every child, is a rich and usually unexamined tapestry of taken-for-granted knowledge about how the world works. (Miller, 1983: 116–119)

## The Individual and Psychoanalysis

And so, just as SLA research gives hints about the subjective experience of the individual, the work of Burkitt, Harré, Mead, and other social theorists is instructive for thinking about persons and their worlds as mutually-informing and mutually-interactive constructions. For, whatever might be the differences between those theorists' conceptualisations of precisely how and when the individual subject or agent is formed, they all acknowledge that individual's existence. They also recognise the importance of communication – specifically language – in the work of creating that individual.

And I do not disagree: the self is constructed in a context in which the social and the linguistic are enmeshed. But I also concur with Ehrman and Dörnyei's contention (1998: 13) that '*intra*-personal processes are an important factor in all *inter*personal processes'. And so I am left curious about how the subject, once created, moves in the world, and especially how it moves within language, and from one language to another. It is, then, this curiosity that demands another discourse, one that works with questions concerning the intra-personal work of the individual in making relations – in and with and through language – between the self and the social nexus, and between different parts of itself. Specifically, Harré's (1993: 3) concept of 'autonomous action', which includes the social work of making meaning, implies that *something* – an individual – is engaged in that work. And if, as Mead (1934) and Burkitt (1991) assert, language is part of what creates and informs the subject, it is also crucial to ask what happens to that created subject when that language – or the linguistic environment – changes. This is a two-pronged question, for while the acquisition of a new language often takes place in a new social or educational context, requiring new interpretation and representation, it is not only the context that changes but also the means (largely linguistic), of interpreting and representing that context to the self.

In directing their gaze primarily at the social, the theories outlined above, like the SLA research cited earlier, do not quite get at that question. Arguably, one discourse that does so is psychoanalysis. Yet curiously, certain ideas from social theory resonate with psychoanalytic concepts. Burkitt, for example, recognises that in lived experience individuals often 'feel divided within themselves' (Burkitt, 1991: 1), even though in his explanation of that phenomenon he rejects what he contends is the Freudian 'dualism between the conscious mind and the emotions' (1991: 21). Further, mirroring the more explicitly psychoanalytic Lacanian view of the self as 'other to itself' (Fink, 1995: 7) that we will later see reflected in the memoirs of Eva Hoffman (1989) and Richard Rodriguez (1988), and in various of the language-learner diaries, is Mead's notion of the self as its own (arguably non-unitary) object. This is expressed in Mead's contention that communication is 'directed not only to others but also to the individual himself' (Mead, 1934: 139). Indeed, though my work is primarily with that 'individual himself' – or herself – the entire discourse of self-and-social, with its emphasis on the importance of language as a means for making identity and engaging in social relations with the world outside of the self, evokes the dialogic structure of psychoanalysis. In particular, it resounds extraordinarily with that branch of psychoanalytic thought known as *object relations theory*, according to which, as will be explored in the next chapter, social relations both inform and are informed by the workings of the individual psyche.

The complex interrelationships among self, culture and language suggest that the learner of a first language, and concomitantly a first culture, is simultaneously engaged in the creation, by means of social and linguistic constructs, of a social and linguistic self. If this is so, second language acquisition is doubly complicated: first, irrespective of the precise level of linguistic (as well as non-linguistic) development of the individual, a *first* self both linguistic and social (albeit labile and always in flux) is, by definition, already in place; second, that self has been and continues to be constructed and re-constructed both socially and linguistically, before, throughout and beyond the second language acquisition process. It seems quite clear, then, that to whatever extent an individual's self-concept emerges from and is informed by the tapestry of the culture in which he or she lives, and is expressed through the first language in which he or she functions, that self must somehow adapt, along with its linguistic and cultural functioning, when the individual enters a new cultural and linguistic environment. But psychical life, described by Lemke (1995: 89) as 'inner dialogue and feelings', also has a part to play in the creation and re-creation of the social self and the relations between that self, the world and the psyche. Indeed, what can 'inner dialogue' mean before there is language?

Perhaps part of what it means is silence. When a psychotherapist says to an analysand, 'I can only work with what you bring me', she is referring not only to the story that is told, but also to the silence that holds back, that resists or refuses telling, or that simply cannot be told because there is no language – or insufficient language – to tell it. Psychoanalytic theory, with its conviction that the greater part of the life of an individual is unknown even to that individual, aims to get at that silence, that unknown, unconscious, hidden dimension, to find a language for it, and to listen to its stories.

For my part, I will endeavour to peel away some of the layers of the second-language learner's silence, to get at some of the stories that that particular silence tells.

## Notes

1. This view refers generally to 'outer' speech – that is, to speech that is observable by other than the speaker – since 'inner speech' in a Vygotskyan sense (1997) is by definition outwardly silent. Nevertheless, as is noted in Chapter 3 with respect to the memoir of Eva Hoffman (1989), it may be that inner speech, too, can be troubled by the second language acquisition process.
2. *The Canadian Oxford Dictionary, s.v.* 'silence'.
3. *American Heritage Dictionary of the English Language,* 3rd edn, *s.v.* 'silence'.

## Chapter 2
# Changing the Subject: Psychoanalytic Theory, Silence and the Self

*Psychoanalysis directs its attention to what cannot be spoken in what is actually being said. It starts from the assumption that there is difficulty in language, that in speaking to others we might be speaking against ourselves, or at least against that part of ourselves which would rather remain unspoken.*
Jaqueline Rose
*The Case of Peter Pan, or*
*The Impossibility of Children's Fiction*, 1984

*That is what is in the beginning –*
*the Promise, not the Word.*
Adam Phillips
*The Beast in the Nursery:*
*On Curiosity and Other Appetites*, 1999

## The Dynamic Self

In the previous chapter I proposed that the lens of psychoanalytic theory might permit a different perspective on the phenomenon of anxiety, as one among many factors in second language acquisition, than second language acquisition research or social theories on their own might allow. In addition, in its ability to expand the scope of what is understood by the term, psychoanalysis may have a helpful contribution to make to an examination of the possibility that one of the manifestations of anxiety, within the second language learning process, may be silence. More broadly, what I ask of psychoanalytic theory in this chapter is to address the problem of how the process of discovery – or creative construction and re-construction – of a self might be understood in the general context of second language acquisition, and within the phenomenon of silence as part of that process. I ask whether the work of acquiring a second language might consist in part of somehow weaving the threads of a new self, a new identity, into the tapestry of the pre-existing one or, perhaps more profoundly, of creating a new 'second-language self' that alters, replaces or coexists with the 'original' one. Does the individual acquiring a second language also acquire, or create, a second world view, perhaps even a second identity? What might this imply for the first world view and the first self?

What clues can silence give us? Could an ambivalent psychical and linguistic silence, a moment when the self is suspended between two languages, be a kind of representation, a *re*-presentation, of a necessary moment of suspension between two linguistic, sociocultural and psychical selves – a place where old and new identities collide, intersect and perhaps eventually engage? Could silence within the process of acquiring a second language be a symptom of, or a defence against, a profound traumatic interference with a former interior self, an *inside*, that is further complicated by the disorienting fact that it takes place in a new or changed *outside* environment? Might there be similarities between early psychical events that distinguish inside from outside, and later disruptions or interferences that re-create those first psychical events? Alternatively, could silence represent the recollection, or the re-experiencing, of an earlier conflict: between inside and outside, or between different aspects of a self, or between different (new and former) selves and their conflicts? What makes creating a self so hard?

And what makes learning so hard? Ehrman and Dörnyei's discussion of the *repetition compulsion phenomenon* which they describe as behaviour patterns that embody 'direct and indirect expression of wishes and impulses, defence mechanisms, and the explanatory cognitions that underlie them' (Ehrman & Dörnyei, 1998: 27) recalls Anna Freud's (1974: 88) insistence that human development consists of 'new editions of very old conflicts'. This claim is itself taken up by Deborah Britzman (1998) and reasserted with respect to learning. 'Learning is a problem', she writes, 'but it has to do with something other than the material of pedagogy ... [For] there to be a learning there must be conflict within learning' (1998: 5). If development is about reliving old conflicts, for Britzman 'learning is a relearning of one's history of learning', and one's history of learning embodies its own conflict 'between the desire to learn and the desire to ignore' (1998: 5). Such conflict is manifested in a complex fashion. The difficulty of making – or failing to make – a connection between the *inside* and the *outside* of the individual, however that individual is defined, is perhaps the most obvious kind of learning conflict, as intimated by Britzman's question, 'What ... happens when the subject that is the learner meets and uses the object that is knowledge?' (Britzman, 1998: 3). But in addition to, and indeed implicit in, that encounter between the inside and the outside that we call learning are the mutually-informing tensions, struggles and collisions between different components of the inside: the self itself.

Britzman's work on conflict in learning looks both broadly and deeply at the interplay between two apparently oppositional internal forces: the wish to learn and the wish to avoid learning, to ignore. These wishes are not conscious intentions. Rather, they are longings rooted in the unconscious, and manifestly both supported and refuted by a crucial quality of the psychical event of learning. Britzman's view that to learn is to relearn, or re-enact, one's history of learning is accompanied by her position that 'it is precisely this unconscious force that renders the work of learning so difficult...' (Britzman, 1998: 5). But how, specifically, might these longings work with and against each other in second language acquisition? What are the old conflicts that must be unlearned, relearned, repeated and re-experienced in the process of acquiring a second language? What happens to selves in conflict? More precisely, what is at stake for the self in the learning of a new language? I turn to a discussion of some of the ways in which psychoanalytic theory considers the self – and the process of creating a self – as sites of conflict and trauma.

Writing about the creating, breaking and remaking of the self abounds in the field of psychoanalytic theory, as it does in other fields within the social sciences. In fact, as the social sciences grow more and more interdisciplinary, there is often a considerable blurring of the boundaries between sociology and social psychology on the one hand (as we have seen with the ideas of Mead, Harré and Burkitt, discussed in the previous chapter) and psychoanalytic thought on the other. The discourses of the former are imbued with the language of the latter: even the terms *conscious* and *unconscious* themselves, along with other concepts, originally psychoanalytical but subsequently metamorphosed and reinterpreted to varying degrees, are frequently part of everyday discourse. Conversely, psychoanalytic theory considers the self, and its vicissitudes, as made and remade, experienced and re-experienced, again and again, in dynamic relation with the world.

Beginning with the work of Sigmund Freud, and forming a supporting framework for a discourse on the psychoanalytic abstractions (anxiety, ambivalence, conflict and loss) that inform this study, are two concepts, themselves integral to the psychoanalytic notion of self: *dynamism* and *relationality*. Among the functions of that part of the self that Freud named *ego* is control over two relation-making activities: first, 'the path to action in regard to the outer world' and, second, 'access to consciousness' (Freud, 1948: 28). In other words, the ego acts as a kind of overseeing intermediary, negotiating relations between internal and external worlds. What is useful to remember is that part of the ego's work is to resist dangers both from within and from without. Alice Pitt and Deborah Britzman trace Freud's evolving conceptualisation of this resistance to its later formulation as 'a defence mounted by the ego so that the ego might continue to enjoy its carefully crafted and, in many ways, useful symptoms' (Pitt & Britzman, forthcoming).

Insofar as language is a function of the ego, it can be understood as one of the ego's ways of performing this negotiating work, this psychical self-defence. Inhibition is, perhaps somewhat paradoxically, another. Writes Freud:

> As regards inhibitions, then, we may say ... that they are restrictions of the functions of the ego which have either been imposed as a measure of precaution or brought about as a result of an impoverishment of energy. (Freud, 1948: 18–19)

What, then, if the ego restricts – or inhibits – language as a defence against the external world? Indeed, could there be a more obvious symptom of inhibited language than silence?

Freud (1948: 16) further describes inhibition as 'the expression of a restriction of an ego-function' that 'differs from a symptom: for a symptom cannot be described as a process that takes place within, or acts upon, the ego' (1948: 19). Rather:

> A symptom arises from an instinctual impulse which has been prejudicially affected by repression. If the ego, by making use of the signal of unpleasure, attains its object of completely suppressing the instinctual impulse, we learn nothing of how this has happened. We can only find out about it from those cases in which repression has ... failed. (Freud: 1948: 26–27)[1]

To bring these ideas to bear on second language acquisition suggests considering silence as a symptom. But what repressed instinctual impulses might silence be symptomatic of? Freud makes two comments that we can take as hints. First he remarks that:

> we are very apt to think of the ego as powerless against the id, but when it is opposed to an instinctual process it has only to give a 'signal of unpleasure' in order to attain its object with the aid of that *almost omnipotent* institution, the *pleasure-principle* (Freud: 1948: 23; my italics).

Second, he maintains that:

> ... most of the repressions with which we have to deal in our therapeutic work are cases of after-expulsion. They presuppose the operation of earlier, primal repressions which exert an attraction on the more recent situation. (Freud: 1948: 25)

The almost omnipotent pleasure principle; primal repressions. How can we think about these in relation to each other? And what connects them both with second language learning? For the ego to function as a mediating force between the inside and the outside, there must *be* an inside and an outside: a self and an other. But such is not the case for the Freudian infant. Rather, two very general ways of considering Freud's notion of self in the very young child are either that there is no self as such, or that the self is all there is. Still, these positions are less contradictory than they appear. For Freud's infant has no sense of itself either as unified or as separate from its world; it begins as a part of the mother from whom it must separate – not just physically but also psychically – before the concept of an individual self can truly apply. There is, for Freud (1948: 109), 'much more continuity between intra-uterine life and earliest infancy' than is suggested by the externally visible separation, at birth, from the mother. And it is owing to this continuity that, although 'during its intra-uterine life the mother was not an object for the foetus, [because] at that time there were no objects at all as far as it was concerned', nevertheless 'the child's biological situation as a foetus is replaced for it by a psychological object-relation to its mother' (Freud, 1948: 109). Prior to this shift, boundaries between the child and the world (the inside and the outside) cannot even be described as undefined, or shifting, since from the perspective of the unindividuated child they simply do not exist at all. The infant has needs, and those needs can be met, but for the infant the objects that meet the needs – a warm, full breast, a soft blanket, a familiar voice – are part of itself. Its wishes imply their own fulfilment, its instincts their own satisfaction. In this state the infant is, in a sense, omnipotent.

## Anxiety, Judgement and Conflict

The undifferentiated, omnipotent state comes to an end in the infant's eventual perception of its mother and itself as dyadic, as other to each other. This perception marks the beginning of the child's work of making distinctions and relations between inside and outside, between self and *not*-self: the beginning of a long personal journey of discovery that will include language, the world, the self and the interrelationships (and the gaps) among them. There is trauma attached to these perceptions. But understood psychoanalytically, according to Jean Laplanche and J.B. Pontalis, trauma by its very nature, as an 'event ... defined by its intensity, by the subject's incapacity to respond adequately to it, and by the upheaval and long-lasting effects that it brings about in the psychical organisation'(Laplanche & Pontalis, 1973: 465), can be assimilated only later. And so, at its originating moment, the event of first separation produces not anxiety as such, but rather a kind of predisposition towards the potential for anxiety:

> The first experience of anxiety through which the individual goes is (in the case of human beings, at all events) birth, and, objectively speaking, birth is a separation from the mother ... Now it would be very satisfactory if anxiety, as a symbol of separation, were to be repeated on every subsequent occasion on which a separation took place. But unfortunately we are prevented from making use of this correlation by the fact that birth is not experienced subjectively as a separation from the mother, since the foetus, being a completely narcissistic creature, is totally unaware of her existence as an object. (Freud, 1948: 94–95)

Birth thus constitutes the infant's first moment of anxiety – or more precisely it *ought* to be, but is not quite, the first moment of anxiety, because it is not subjectively experienced by the infant. For Freud (1948: 104–105) 'the earliest phobias of infancy cannot be directly traced back to impressions of birth'. He explains: 'A certain preparedness for anxiety is undoubtedly present in the infant. But this preparedness ... does not emerge till later on, as the mental development of the infant proceeds' (Freud, 1948: 105) and it becomes aware of, and perceives as a 'danger ... against which it wants to be safeguarded', the possibility of 'non-gratification, of a growing tension due to need, against which it is helpless' (1948: 106–107). Perhaps what is key here is that, regardless of exactly when danger is first perceived by the Freudian infant, the response to that danger is anxiety. And anxiety, says Freud, is manifested in three circumstances – when a child is alone, in the dark, or with an unknown person:

> [T]hese three instances can be reduced to a single condition, namely, that of missing someone who is loved and longed-for. Here is the key, I think, to an understanding of anxiety and to a reconciliation of the contradictions that seem to beset it ... [Now] it seems as though the longing turns into anxiety. This anxiety has all the appearance of the child's feeling of not knowing what to do, as though in its still undeveloped state it did not know how to cope with its cathexis of longing. Here anxiety seems to be a reaction to the felt loss of the object; and one is at once reminded of the fact ... that the earliest anxiety of all – the primal anxiety of birth – is brought about on the occasion of a separation from the mother. (Freud, 1948: 105–106)

Whether or not it is birth that precisely marks the first moment of anxiety, it seems that the child's later perception of its separation from its mother as 'dangerous' recalls something about the moment, or the process, of birth that gave rise to the possibility of that later perception. This later perception and the recalling of the earlier moment that facilitated it are not conscious acts, but rather psychical events – perhaps the first psychical events – that mark the beginning of what Britzman calls the 'ego's work of mediating and distinguishing inside and outside pressures' (Britzman, 1998: 138 fn. 5).

The anxiety that the perception of danger produces is, in Freud's words, an 'affective state and as such can, of course, only be felt by the ego [while the] id cannot have anxiety as the ego can; for it is not an organisation and cannot make a judgment about a situation of danger' (Freud, 1948: 113). The id cannot make a judgement, but the ego can. And coincident with these first inside–outside distinctions is the first Freudian judgement:

> Expressed in the language of the oldest – the oral – instinctual impulses, the judgment is: 'I should like to eat this', or 'I should like to spit it out'; and, put more generally: 'I should like to take this into myself and to keep that out'. That is to say: 'It shall be inside me' or 'It shall be outside me' ... [The] original pleasure-ego wants to introject into itself every-thing that is good and to eject from itself everything that is bad. What is bad, what is alien to the ego and what is external are, to begin with, iden-tical. (Freud, 1925: 439)

Two curious parallels, crucial for my own theorising, arise from Freud's rendering of the concept of the first judgement in terms of orality. First, I find compelling the resonance between, on one hand, early orality as it refers to 'eating and spitting out' and, on the other hand, the later relation-ship of language to orality. Adam Phillips' observation resonates likewise:

> Breathing, eating, babbling, singing, and speaking make a puzzling continuum of experience; we are always at, or on, the oral stage wherever else we are. What kind of meals does the child make of words? (Phillips, 1999: 62)

Second, Freud's speculation concerning the indistinguishability, in this early self, between the bad, the alien and the external, invites thinking about ways in which a second language, also external and alien, might like-wise be judged bad. Taken together, these parallels lend support to my suggestion that there might be some relation between the early psychical events that allow (or require) the individual to begin to make the distinc-tion between what is inside and what is outside – between self and other – and later events that in some way recall those earlier ones.

In his discussion of childhood sexual curiosity, Phillips asserts that, for the Freudian child, 'Words are his route back to bodies' (Phillips, 1999: 29).

For this discussion, there is perhaps a way in which, in an inversion of Phillips' comment, thinking about bodies may lead us back to words. Might we think about second language acquisition as a similar kind of judgement, that is, a judgement on the part of the learning subject about whether the second language is something to be taken in or kept out of the self? Indeed, these metaphorical similarities between early judgement and second language acquisition hint at an illuminating way to imagine a moment, or a period, of silence: to refuse to eat, and likewise to refuse to speak, I must merely shut my mouth.

A being that is complete and omnipotent, in the sense that it perceives itself as the world and the world as part of itself, embodies no conflict. There are needs within that being, but they are met. That is all: simply put, there is nothing to fight about. But for Freud the individual that emerges from the traumatic experience of separation from the mother is, as noted above, one who has distinguished 'good' from 'bad' in order to enact the separation by taking in one and rejecting the other, and who unconsciously equates the former with the *self* and the latter with *not-self*, with that which is other.

This distinction between good and bad marks the very beginning of what Freud refers to as the genesis of love and hate as opposing forces and, significantly for this project, ambivalence and conflict. This is so even though love and hate originate differently (love as an originally narcissistic urge for pleasure that has been transferred onto objects, and hate as derived from the early 'narcissistic ego's primordial repudiation of the [*bad* aspects of the] external world' [Freud, 1915a, 136–137]). We begin to grasp the implications of this shift in perception – this coming to behold, on the part of the infant, its mother's and concomitantly its own otherness – when we consider that the process of individuation is experienced by the child (though not assimilated until later) as the traumatic loss of the omnipotence that was formerly embodied within its primal sense of unity, that unity which made all needs satisfiable and all wishes possible. The child, no longer containing the world but now contained both in and by it, is quite literally dis-ordered, its former being deranged, silenced, replaced (and yet not forgotten) by a new, separate self. This is the first separation, the first loss of an earlier (because unseparated) self, the first moment of anxiety.

## Loss, Mourning and Melancholia

The next 'transformation of anxiety' named by Freud is 'the castration anxiety belonging to the phallic phase, [which is] also a fear of separation'

(Freud, 1948: 109). He argues that, because the genitalia represent the possibility of reunification with the mother:

> being separated from [one's genitals] amounts to a renewed separation from [one's mother] and this in turn means being helplessly exposed to an unpleasurable tension due to instinctual need, as was the case in birth. (Freud, 1948: 110)

But the oral and phallic stages intertwine. And in addition to their symbolic resonance *vis-à-vis* the mother, and separation from her, the genitals are an important source of physical pleasure for the infant. So is the mouth. And the acquisition of language coincides temporally – albeit with substantial variation in the degree of overlap – with the physical separation of mother and child through weaning as well as with the infant's growing awareness of its mother as other to itself. If it can be argued, then, that the fear of castration echoes the fear of separation from the mother, it follows that language acquisition might be similarly experienced by the child as somehow connected with, or transferred to, the disruption of oral pleasure. To separate from the mother is, in a crucial sense, to lose her as an object. But it is also to lose that previous and precious version of one's own self that, in a sense, contained the mother.

It is as a second instantiation of loss and separation that Phillips (1999) articulates both the making of a speaking self out of a non-speaking one, and the corresponding loss, on acquiring language, of the previous, inarticulate self. Phillips neatly connects, on the one hand, the concept of loss as paradoxically and even painfully accompanying the process of maturation (which begins with the first traumatic separation) with, on the other hand, the acquisition of language. It is an odd idea, that acquiring a new language might, in some sense, constitute a loss. But Phillips explains:

> Through the displacement and substitution of her desires, the child is all the time giving things up – omnipotence, desire for and dominion over the parents, babbling – in order to secure the supposedly more viable satisfactions of maturity, all of which entail increasingly sophisticated forms of representation. (Phillips, 1999: 39)

Later, he probes more deeply this issue of loss, specifically with respect to language learning:

> Learning to talk is difficult, and it doesn't get any easier. The child at nursery school is at that age when he or she is making for the first, but not the last, time that fateful transition – that can never be complete, that can never be whole-hearted because *the renunciation, the loss of the unspoken*

*self is too great* – to joining the language group, to participating in the community of apparently competent speakers. 'Why are words the thing?' the child might wonder, if it could ... *Or, to ask a more obviously psychoanalytic question, what exactly must be given up in order to speak?* (Phillips, 1999: 43; my italics)

Phillips' examination of what is at risk in 'joining the language group' – an action that on its face seems patently desirable – is paradoxically relevant to a discussion of the traumatic aspects of the moment, or the process, of one's initial individuation. For each gain is accompanied by a loss: Freud's infant, in separating from the mother, gains independence at the expense of omnipotence, and Phillips' language learner gains access to the world of speech but loses that earlier unspoken, unspeaking, and unspeakable, self. Phillips is splendidly articulate on this point:

Children around nursery age – between two and three years old – are both just learning to speak and just making the momentous transition from family to the first version of school. And one thing this entails, among many others, is a paradoxical form of renunciation for the child. At the time when her curiosity is becomingly increasingly sophisticated, it is as though she has to give up what she can never in fact relinquish, her inarticulate self, the self before language ... At this point in her life the child leaves more than one home, something she will do every time she speaks, which is always out of her own previous silence. That noisy silence, before language joined in, is a lengthy part of her own history. Words are not merely a substitute for wordlessness; they are something else entirely. (Phillips, 1999: 42–43)

The initial transition, from omnipotent, undifferentiated infant to individuated self, is thus echoed in the transition from unspeaking to speaking individual. And the loss, and the traumatic aspects of that loss, are echoed too: relived in a sense, or perhaps unconsciously remembered as they resound throughout the remnants of that earlier self, the self that existed before the transition that Phillips suggests 'can never be whole-hearted because the renunciation, the loss of the unspoken self is too great' (Phillips, 1999: 43). I take the position, with Phillips, that in the case of the first language (L1) learner the object that is lost, and whose loss is not consciously known to the subject, is the pre-language self.

Such profound losses, however incomplete the renunciations that give rise to them, must be mourned. This is another implication of the initial making of a self as separate from an other, an inside set apart from the outside. Freud posits both mourning and the distinct but related process of melancholia as potential consequences of the shattering of an object-relation – the loss of, or disappointment by, a love-object (Freud, 1917: 257). Specifically, he describes mourning as 'the reaction to the loss of a loved person, or to the loss of some abstraction which has taken the place of one, such as one's country, liberty, an ideal, and so on' (1915: 251–52). But what is of additional interest to me in the present context is Freud's application of this idea of loss to melancholia. It seems that what is at stake in melancholia is

> a loss of a more ideal kind ... [in which the individual] cannot consciously perceive what he has lost either. This might be so even if the patient is aware of the loss which has given rise to his melancholia, but only in the sense that he knows *whom* he has lost but not *what* he has lost in him. (Freud, 1915: 253–54; italics in original)

What if language learning, in the sense that it involves a loss of a former, pre-language self, and by implication second language learning as a transformation from first-language self into second-language self, were considered as a process parallel to those that Freud names mourning and melancholia? In this theoretical model, the lost or disappointing object would be neither a loved person nor an idea as such. Rather, it would be part of an individual's own unconscious – the aspect of the self that is lost either in the transformation from non-speaking to speaking self or, in the case of the shift from first to second language shift, in the movement from one language to the second. Might the learning that provokes the transformation be itself a shattering force? Could the psychical activity of learning (including language learning) insofar as it involves both an encounter between the external and the internal in their various aspects and the consequent loss of some aspect of the internal, invoke a process not unlike mourning and – depending on the degree of the disruption – even approach melancholia?

A close reading of Freud's conceptual analysis of melancholia is helpful to this discussion, but a cautionary word is needed first. For many reasons it seems counter-intuitive, peculiar, even disturbing, to think about the second language acquisition process as a mental disorder, or to think about any part of that process as pathological. Nor is that what I want to do. But it is important to remember that one of Freud's methods of working with ideas about the mind is to consider the pathological as a kind of hinting at the normal. My discussion here is not intended to pathologise the silent period or any other aspect of second language learning, nor is it to preclude or dismiss any other, non-psychoanalytic reading of silence. Rather, I aim to invite reflection on Freud's view of the pathology of melancholia in order to move a little bit behind the notion of the silent period as a transparent phenomenon, into a consideration of some of the potentially significant implications of the second-language learner's silence. I want to ask: why silence? Can thinking about silence as a symptom help us to think about acquiring a second language as a process that is sometimes, for some learners, also a problem?

The analysis of mourning put forward in Freud's (1917) essay on *Mourning and Melancholia* can be briefly and generally summed up thus: when an object (most commonly a person) loved by the subject ceases to exist, the subject's libidinal energy – what we might call its psychical attention – must be withdrawn from its attachment to that object. But this presents a difficulty for the subject, who does not want to withdraw from its object; such withdrawal is painful, both in itself and because it requires the full admission that the object is gone. Although reality ultimately rules the day, and the necessary withdrawal comes to pass, the process can nevertheless be a long and slow one, during which the object is 'psychically prolonged' (Freud, 1917: 251) on the part of the subject.

Situated in a kind of connected contraposition to mourning is melancholia, where, as indicated above, the loss is more ideal – that is, it is not that the object has truly ceased to exist, but rather that it has become, in some sense, lost to the subject: for Freud '[the] object has not perhaps actually died, but has been lost as an object of love' (Freud, 1917: 253). It may even be that the subject knows only that *something* has been lost, but does not know what that something is. For Freud, this suggests that in melancholia the object-loss is 'withdrawn from consciousness, in contradistinction to mourning, in which there is nothing about the loss that is unconscious' (1917: 254). Further, Freud maintains, an additional symptom of melancholia not present in mourning is:

> an extraordinary diminution in [the subject's] self-regard, an impoverishment of his ego on a grand scale. In mourning it is the world which has become poor and empty; in melancholia it is the ego itself. (Freud, 1917: 254)

There is an interesting reverberation between this idea of ego impoverishment on the one hand, and the inadequacies of language on the other (particularly, though not only, before it is fully acquired), that returns us to Phillips' (1999: 43) idea that something must be given up in order to learn to speak. If, in the progressivist view, the aim of the subject's newly attained ability to speak and be understood is simply to fill an empty, linguistically-silent self that preceded it, then with language acquisition nothing is truly lost, for the former pre-language self contained nothing to lose. But, for Phillips, to argue that the pre-language self is empty is incorrect; the silent *nothing* that language replaces is in fact *something*. Thus, if the pre-language self can be understood as incomplete or diminished, so can that of the newly-speaking subject which, as Phillips argues, must relocate, or relearn, that important and irreplaceable non-speaking part of itself:

> ... [It] is not quite clear what the limits of language are limits of. So in a progressivist view of education we would say: the child must learn to speak, to communicate his need. In a nonprogressivist view we would have to add: *the child* (and the adult) *must learn not to speak, must remember what that is like; must be shown how speaking comes out of the unspeaking part of ourselves*. The young child will be taught to speak, because he will also notice – or acknowledge through his determined disregard – that there are areas of experience, realms of feeling, that seem resistant to speech, where words might seem inappropriate or ill-suited. (Phillips, 1999: 44; my italics)

For Phillips, then, the speaking self mourns the loss of the unspeaking part of itself. But there is more. For the subject is always in relation with both itself and its other – that is, what is outside of itself. And so the newly-speaking self, constantly encouraged and even required to communicate, is having impressed upon it at every turn the utter impossibility of full communication, because what it cannot communicate is its *un*speaking.

For a second-language learner, in an L2 environment, the experience is further complicated. The primal, nonspeaking or unspeaking self is, by its nature, un*speak*able (though nonetheless present as a kind of echo or shadow), and the first-language-speaking self is diminished because it is, at best, not understood and, at worst, regarded by its new linguistic other as not worthy of understanding. At the same time it is being subjected to all the misrecognitions imaginable in the complex web of relations between inside and outside. Freud (1917) asserts that melancholia can include 'a lowering of the self-regarding feelings to a degree that finds utterance in self-reproaches and self-revilings'. Later, he describes it as manifested in 'the patient [in a state of melancholia] represent[ing] his ego to [the psycho-analyst] as worthless, incapable of any achievement and morally despicable'. And later still, Freud makes the claim that:

> the essential thing, therefore, is not whether the melancholic's distressing self-denigration is correct ... the point must rather be that *he is giving a correct description of his psychological situation ... what he tells us points to a loss in regard to his ego*. (Freud, 1917: 252–256; my italics).

All these statements share in common an assumption of the ability to articulate; it is quite axiomatic to say that for representations of melancholia to be made *to* someone, the ability to represent must be present. But consider the language learner. To whatever extent she or he might possess Freud's lowered self-regard and disrupted ego, those difficulties are accompanied in both first-language and second-language learners by a lack of sufficient linguistic competence to represent that diminished self-regard. The former is not competent in any language, and the latter is proficient only in a language that has little or no purchase in the current context – what kind of reading of silence within the process of SLA, then, do these statements of Freud's invite? Might silence be, in part, a non-response – which by definition is the only response the self, the ego, can make, to its own accusations?

Freud's discussion of melancholia goes on to state that, rather than corresponding to the melancholic subject, the self-accusations of the melancholic might rather correspond to someone the subject 'loves or has loved or should love' and be 'reproaches against a loved object which have been shifted away from it onto the patient's own ego' (Freud, 1917: 257). This psychoanalytic statement warrants exploration within the context of the language learner.

But it is a tricky claim even in its own world; to attempt engagement with it in the context of language acquisition is to invite interpretive labour of a kind with which Freud might not be uncomfortable, but many others would. Once more, it seems worthwhile to reiterate that I undertake this speculation in precisely that spirit: to play more than to pathologise, to conjecture rather than conclude.

What, then, can we infer, from Freud's assessment concerning melancholia, about the experience of the language learner? Whom, or what, has he or she loved, but loves no longer: whom, or what, should he or she be loving? And to whom might he or she be reproachful? It seems that to ask these questions is to imply that what is at stake in language learning is fundamentally the relationships that individuals make, not only with language but also with the world and, most significantly of all, with (or within) themselves. For if we acknowledge the mutability of the self, and take as given the Lacanian proclamation that the self is other to itself (Fink, 1995: 7), the idea that the first- or second-language learner can be engaged in a struggle with (and thus perhaps reproach, or cease to love) her or his former self, be it pre-linguistic or first-language-speaking, is not unthinkable. Nor does it require a huge leap to consider that the self, in this Freudian context, might 'reproach' what can only be a former version of itself, its own ego prior to the current process of transformation.

Something that might prove to be a little trickier is the consideration of what, precisely, the earlier self is being accused of: that is, what is it being reproached for? For it seems to me that it is not simply the (earlier version of the) self as such that is being struggled against by the newer, language-acquiring version, but also the self's representation of itself or, more accurately, its inability to represent itself. This may be what is most intolerable to the individual acquiring language who cannot even recognise, much less articulate, the un-representable aspects of either the language acquisition process or the versions of the self that preceded and resulted from that process. Put another way, the self in transition from no-language to language, or the self in transition between first and second languages, can know the need for, but is in a very important sense unable to articulate, its reproaches. For although the individual may have inferred, from all externally-originating efforts to change it, that the old means of self-representation is no longer sufficient to maintain the relation between inside and outside, the new form of representation is as yet not entirely acquired.

What shatters the language learner's relationship with the object that is, or was, the pre-language omnipotent self, or the first language not-quite-omnipotent-but-nevertheless-expressive self, is the learning that a new language, a new means of expression, is called for. But, as Ehrman and Dörnyei (1998: 185) point out, individuals may resist learning, and they may do so through silence, because learning 'requires rejection of one's own deficiency'. That is to say that hand in hand with learning that one needs a new language goes the inference that the old language (or the pre-language state), and therefore the former version of the self, which lived either without language or with*in* the first language, are no longer sufficient – are even, somehow, wrong.[2] This learning – this shattering – echoes an earlier learning, an earlier disruption, namely the realisation of the self's separateness (and the corresponding inadequacy of the unseparated self) from its mother. And further, much as that earlier realisation marked a kind of loss of the previous self (perceived as united with the mother), the acknowledgement of the need to revise the first-language self to include a second language which it now needs to make itself known – even when there is no loss of the mother tongue as such – is a reminder of the loss of the mother as part of the self. Thus the self disappoints itself.

This story of loss and separation, from an earlier self imagined as more or less omnipotent, is the story of a wish and its sublimation. For Freud, it is the first wish, the primal urge towards unmitigated pleasure that informs early unconscious mental processes: 'these processes strive towards gaining pleasure; psychical activity draws back from any event which might arouse unpleasure' (Freud, 1911: 36). These primary processes, Freud claims, are disturbed by the intervention of reality. The reality-ego

interrupts the pleasure-ego: the desire for what is useful ultimately subli-
mates the urge for immediate pleasure. Still:

> the substitution of the reality principle for the pleasure principle implies
> no deposing of the pleasure principle, but only a safeguarding of it. A
> momentary pleasure, uncertain in its results, is given up, but only in
> order to gain along the new path an assured pleasure at a later time.
> (Freud, 1911: 40–41)

Phillips (1999: 42) looks on language as mediating the longings and
desires that had their home originally in the 'self before language, ... [the]
passionate life without words'. As the child acquires language and the concomitant pleasures and usefulness of communication, she must surrender
the imagined omnipotence of the pre-speech life in which language was not
needed: she must give up the pleasures of speechlessness.

That speechlessness might involve pleasure, rather than (or in addition
to) frustration at the inability to communicate, seems at first counter-
intuitive. But let us recall that the pleasures that psychoanalytic theory
refers to, and which for Phillips (1999: 39) constitute exactly what must be
given up in order for the child to mature, include 'omnipotence, desire for
and dominion over the parents, babbling'. It is those pleasures whose 'displacement and substitution' by the 'desires for satisfaction ... are assumed
to be, one way or another, driving the child into the future'.

Thus, despite what is gained by acquiring language, the old longing for
omnipotence is not completely repressed: it does not die, and furthermore
it is re-awakened, or remembered, or even re-experienced, in the acquisition of a second language. This is so not only because of the longing for the
omnipotence of the previous, pre-language state, but also because, with
respect to the L2 environment and relative to that second language, the self
that has not yet acquired it is, in effect, without speech. That is, as the primal
unspeaking infant is to the speaking child, so is the self of the first language
to its later manifestation as speaker of the second language. Although the
stakes are somewhat different in second language acquisition – the self has
already sublimated its omnipotence fantasy – what is paralleled is the
reluctant relinquishing of a previous linguistic potency. And the disappointment of this later disruption recalls the earlier one.

## Ambivalence: Holding On, Letting Go

Still, it is important not to forget that there is more to the acquisition of a
second (or for that matter, a first) language than simply disappointment.
There are real gains, and real pleasures, to be found in joining a community

of speakers. The primal wish for omnipotence may persist, and powerfully, but in the end it is only a wish. And from the first time the infant's cry for the breast was not immediately answered, the reality that has engendered the formation of an individuated self has likewise been informing that self of the impossibility of attaining its wish. For Freud, the reality ego acts specifically, according to its principle, to protect the self against the unpleasure that accompanies the unsatisfiable wish (Freud, 1911: 40-41). Language seems to be one of reality's responses to the question of how wishes can be fulfilled. And every attempt to provide an answer, however partial such an answer might be, is an acknowledgement of the question. Thus, not only does reality conflict with the wish for omnipotence, but in addition, reality's response to this conflict between itself and the wish (namely, in this discussion, the insistence that the subject acquire a language) might be a source of ambivalence. This is because accepting this response and acting on that acceptance requires a further letting go of the omnipotence wish – here, precisely, the wish not to need language. If we recast the following statement, substituting 'learning' for 'love', perhaps we begin to hint at this: 'the loss of a love-object is an excellent opportunity for the ambivalence in love-relationships to make itself effective and come into the open' (Freud, 1917: 260).

In second language learning, I have argued, the love-object (or the learning-object) that is lost is the first-language self: specifically, the self that could make itself known, to the world and to itself, in its first language. I now advance the view that silence in the second language acquisition process might be, on two levels, a manifestation of the subject's ambivalence surrounding the learning that accompanies that loss. First, there is the wish to avoid the unpleasure of having its needs misread, misunderstood and consequently unsatisfied, as against the acknowledgement of the first-language self's incapacity to avoid that unpleasure. Second, there is the profound admission that one's position in any language is a reluctant abandonment of a not-quite-forgotten position of imagined omnipotence in the 'passionate life without words' (Phillips, 1999: 42).

Looked at in this light, ambivalence may be one of the mildest of possible consequences of this loss of an earlier self, which surely is potentially quite profound. And to the extent that the self is made by unconscious processes, by negotiations between the inside and the outside of the individual, might the loss that accompanies learning (when that learning is itself disruptive) be a painful dislocation? Might it be a grievous derangement of the unconscious, the restoration of which becomes potentially as difficult as that of the ego in the melancholic, even despite the gains that are made (for and by the self) through the acquisition of language? If learning 'requires rejection of one's own deficiency' (Ehrman & Dörnyei, 1998: 185), then every learning is in some sense a loss, a rupture, for it carries the insinuation that the self – that is, the self before the learning – was imperfect, lesser somehow, than the self that is re-created from it. As Britzman (1998: 11) puts it, part of what education does is to ask the learner 'to confront perspectives, situations, and ideas that may not be just unfamiliar but appear at first glance as a criticism of [his or her] view'. How better, then, to avoid acknowledging the losses at stake in moving into another language than to hesitate or refuse to do so? And since, in this case, what is at stake is simultaneously the means of *telling the story of what is at stake*, what could make more sense as a way of refusing, however unconsciously, to take the position that admits the loss, than simply to keep silent?

This is but one more place in which thinking about the relationship between language and the self becomes tricky. For language functions uniquely. In addition to being a 'knowledge' (in and of itself, about the world and the self), it is also, in a certain sense, a methodology. It serves to communicate other knowledges, other desires, to interpret understanding and ignorance and, crucially for the present discussion, to create, re-create, communicate, interpret, present and represent the self, both to the world and to the self. Thus a study of language acquisition can, arguably, be muddied and muddled in ways that an examination of other kinds of learning might not be. A brief look at the work of Jacques Lacan may provide a little insight into this messiness.

To engage, even briefly, with Lacan's thinking on language and alienation is to begin to wonder about some of the ways in which, even as individuals make selves within, and out of (and even despite ) language, language circumscribes those individuals and the selves they make. Of course, language also circumscribes the discourses we can have, including those about language in general, and about second language acquisition in particular. And language hints at itself, and at its own circumscription: writes Fink, in his work on Lacanian theory:

> The very expression we use to talk about it – 'mother tongue' – is indicative of the fact that it is some Other's tongue first, the mOther's tongue, that is, the mOther's language, and in speaking of childhood experience, Lacan often virtually equates the Other with the mother. (Fink, 1995: 7)

The very idea of one's language as belonging, at first, to this 'mOther' adds another dimension to the already-complex earlier discussion of the mother–child relation, which is ruptured, in a psychoanalytic sense, as the infant begins to apprehend its mother as other to itself. And yet for Lacan, the problem of the individual attempting to make a self within language is even more complex, and lies even deeper: within the otherness of language itself. In his analysis of Lacan's 'Other' Fink remarks that, according to Lacan:

> We are born into a world of discourse, a discourse or language that precedes our birth and that will live on long after our death ... [Children's] wants are, however, moulded in that very process [of language], for the words they are obliged to use are not their own and do not necessarily correspond to their own particular demands: their very desires are cast in the mould of the language or languages they learn ... Though widely considered innocuous and purely utilitarian in nature, language brings with it a fundamental form of alienation that is part and parcel of learning *one's mother tongue*. (Fink, 1995: 5–7; italics in original)

Fink further reminds us that, for Lacan, language is an enormous problem. Though initially the above passage reads very much like a summation of the concept of linguistic determinism, which at present holds relatively little currency, Lacan's concern seems to be more with the idea that all language, as a signifying system, is an alienating and falsifying medium. In that conceptualisation of alienation, maintains Fink (1996: 76–77), the child must make the 'forced choice' to submit to the other that is language because that is the only way 'to be represented by words', even though words are themselves a kind of 'distorting medium or straitjacket'. The child who chooses against this submission effectively foregoes the possibility of subjectivity: the one who submits 'becomes one of language's subjects ... [and in] coming to be as a divided subject, disappears beneath or behind the signifier' – that is, language. If, for Lacan, the acquisition of a language is part of what makes the self other to itself, what might the acquisition of a second language do? Does it affirm the self's alienation from itself with a snide linguistic elbow in the ribs? Does it recall the first forced choice of language? Or does it recall, reawaken, re-articulate the primal longing for subjectivity that was both met and refused by language?

Still, if language is other to the self, as Lacan would have it, it is also, simultaneously, part of the self. Though language circumscribes individuals it is nonetheless one of the principal ways in which those circumscribed individuals present themselves to the world, and in addition to themselves. It may not be enough, but it is what we have – and at the same time it may be what we have, but it is not enough. Recasting his concept of the 'good-enough mother' in the mould of language, psychoanalyst Donald Winnicott might ask: is it good enough? And following Winnicott, part of what I am asking is what happens when language is *not* good enough.

Like Freud and Phillips, Winnicott (1990) has a great deal to say about the concept of the self as a unit that can be ruptured, for good or ill, by various means. With Phillips, Winnicott is among those whose work intersects with the branch of psychoanalytic thought known as *object relations theory*, which places relationship at the foundation and the forefront of the individual's work of making, and the continual shifting and changing of, identity. Winnicott holds the view that, as part of the process of identity development, 'the infant separates out objects and then the environment from the self', becoming a unit that allows for 'a complex interchange between what is inside and what is outside... [an interchange which] constitutes the main relationship of the individual to the world' (Winnicott, 1963b, 72). Language is one of the chief means by which these relationships are enacted. What, then, might it signify to the relationships to rupture the means? Conversely, if somehow the relationships are broken, what might happen to the language that mediates the connection between the 'outside' world and the 'inside' self? Might either or both fractures be manifested in inhibited learning, anxiety, or a defence through silence?

Winnicott's article, *Sum, I Am*, focuses on his idea that 'the central feature in human development is the arrival and secure maintenance of the stage of I AM' (Winnicott, 1963a: 56). Human beings are born with 'inherited tendencies towards growth and development' (1963a: 62), but achieving the stage of recognition that one is a being separate from other beings is a process that can be interrupted if something crucial is lacking in, or taken abruptly from, the child's environment. For Winnicott, the child's dependence on the human environment, complete at infancy, gradually diminishes, both because the child's needs decrease and because the people in the environment grow less able to read those needs. Nevertheless, if a child is to be healthy, the environment in early life must be reliable. Elsewhere Winnicott (1970: 119) advances the idea that the attainment of personal identity 'can only become fact in each individual case because of good-enough mothering and environmental provision of the holding variety'.

If attaining personal identity requires a kind of environmental holding in addition to actual, physical holding on the part of the caregiver, where, precisely, is this holding to come from? For Winnicott:

> gradually a child values being let go, and this corresponds with the presentation to the child of the Reality Principle, which at first clashes with the Pleasure Principle (omnipotence abrogated). The family continues this holding, and society holds the family. (Winnicott, 1961: 107)

Might language, as other to the child – and indeed as one of the ways in which the child learns of her or his own otherness – be part of what constitutes this environmental kind of holding? Might we draw a parallel between the verbal soothing that caregivers tend to give troubled children as they grow older (as opposed to the actual physical holding of infancy and early childhood) and Winnicott's environmental holding?

For Winnicott (1967: 28), the consequence of adequate environmental holding is 'a continuity of existence that becomes a sense of existing, a sense of self, and eventually results in autonomy'. What, then, is the result of holding that is not adequate? If an individual's mother tongue metaphorically holds that individual in the environment, offering a kind of linguistic security, what happens when the linguistic environment undergoes a fundamental shift, and the mother tongue is no longer 'good enough'? Might holding *by* the mother tongue become a silencing, a holding, *of* the tongue?

Winnicott's mention of the pleasure and reality principles that help to ground psychoanalytic thought brings this discussion back to Freud's writing on melancholia, in which:

> owing to a real slight or disappointment ... the object-relationship was shattered ... [and] an object-loss was transformed into an ego-loss and the conflict between the ego and the loved person into a cleavage between the critical activity of the ego and the ego as altered by identification. (Freud, 1917: 258)

In my reading of this statement, in the context of language acquisition, the lost object for the child acquiring language is her or his pre-language omnipotence – or more accurately the longing for omnipotence. This object-loss transforms into an ego-loss: the self that was unconsciously understood to contain the world and to be omnipotent is gone. What is left might tentatively be called a kind of omni-*im*potence. It is not quite nameable by the child, partly because of the incipiency of his or her facility in language and partly because of the otherness of language itself, which can never, regardless of facility, articulate the pre-language self. The child cannot express this loss, and indeed, because of its inexpressibility, is not even aware of it.

In second language acquisition, the experience repeats itself. This is, of course, not to say that the two processes are identical, but rather that in several important aspects they can be thought about similarly. First, both the child acquiring a first language and the second-language learner are discovering, or rediscovering, their own otherness: the former to his or her caregivers and to the world, the latter to a new linguistic environment. Second, in both cases the self that existed prior to the discovery – however mutable and however inexpressible it might have been given the limitations of language – is altered by that discovery. The alteration comprises a loss or a sublimation that cannot be articulated. This point bears emphasising. For it is true that, with relatively few exceptions, in the case of the second-language learner the first language is retained and continues to be used. But though we might conclude from this that the second language acquisition process ceases to resemble that of first language acquisition, psychoanalytic theory invites a position that argues for the retention of the pre-language self and, further, for its continued existence no matter how many languages are ultimately acquired. Moreover, it must be remembered that, even though the second-language learner's L1 self is retained, it too embodies the inexpressible memory of itself before language. Thus, to whatever extent the individual acquiring a second language might arguably be able to express the L1 self, she is nevertheless, like the first-language learner, unable to articulate that still-earlier self.

But again, what about silence? I am once more compelled to return to Freud's disquisition on melancholia, which he insists can include 'a lowering of the self-regarding feelings to a degree that *finds utterance in self-reproaches and self-revilings*' (Freud, 1917: 252; my italics). This assertion invites – even urges – us to acknowledge the possibility that, for some individuals in the process of acquiring a second language, the nature of the process itself might result in self-regarding feelings being lowered to an even greater degree: a moment in which the ego, to extend Freud's phrase, *cannot even find that utterance.*

Is it possible for a person to be utterly unable to speak? Can the tongue become tied so tightly? Perhaps we have known a toddler who cries from frustration, or whose tantrums appear to 'come out of nowhere' and yet transform a tiny body into an explosion of feelings that are clearly profound but, for a young child just beginning to acquire language, inexpressible by verbal means. Or perhaps we have observed, or experienced, non-verbal therapies such as art therapy, in which clients are frequently unable at first to talk about their creations but may gradually arrive at significant verbal explanation or expression of them, as well as other aspects of their experience. If so, we may have an inkling of the power of the inarticulate. If 'words are [the child's] route back to bodies' (Phillips, 1999: 29), then bodies are what there are before there are words. And bodies can also be the place to which wordlessness, as lived by the learner of a second language, might sometimes take us back. For although older children and adults (who in second second language acquisition contexts are socialised against it, or have repressed their anger enough to preclude it) cannot have tantrums in public, they can surely hold their tongues.

And sometimes they do. It may not be the case that all second-language learners undergo a silent period. Likewise, it may not be that all silences in SLA occur exclusively, or at all, for the reasons I have named. But I offer this possibility: that the silent period in some second-language learners might be a kind of psychical paralysis, a temporary freezing,[3] a complex combination of an inability to articulate and a lowered self-regard. And perhaps this possibility offers us a way to imagine silence as symptomatic of the loss, ambivalence and conflict that accompany a transition between two languages, a psychical suspension between two selves. Silence may thus constitute one response to the encounter between a complicated inside and an incomprehensible and uncomprehending outside.

I conclude this chapter by referring briefly to the concept of *liminality*, as described by Carolyn Heilbrun in a series of lectures on women figures in English literature. It seems to speak meaningfully to the idea that stands at the heart of this project:

> The word 'limen' means 'threshold', and to be in a state of liminality is to be poised upon uncertain ground, to be leaving one condition or country or self and entering upon another. But the most salient sign of liminality is its unsteadiness, its lack of clarity about exactly where one belongs and what one should be doing, or wants to be doing. (Heilbrun, 1999: 3)

The self suspended between languages is a liminal self, living unsteadily in two languages and therefore living fully in neither, for whom silence might be not only a symptom of its liminality, but also at least a partial answer to the questions about where that self belongs. Later, when Heilbrun (1999: 37) refers to liminality as a state embodying what Marina Warner (1981: 23) first named 'irreconcilable oppositions' (a quality of ambiguity that allows an individual to 'span opposites'), she might well be speaking of the second-language learner, positioned on the blurred borderline between first and second languages, unable either to turn back and regain the old self or to move forward, unencumbered, into a new one. I turn now to an engagement with some of those selves and their experiences of loss, ambivalence and liminality.

## Notes

1. For Freud (1915c: 153), the psychical mechanism of repression is motivated by 'nothing else than the avoidance of unpleasure'. If that mechanism should fail, unpleasure is certain to result. Freud's statement here that we can only know about this unpleasure (and by extension the incompleteness of the repression that sought to avoid it) after the repression has failed, hints at the concept of *Nachträglichkeit*, or deferred action. This concept will be useful in my discussion,

in the following chapters, of the writing and interpretation of narratives in the form of memoirs and language-learner diaries.

2. Riley's paper on the identity of the bilingual child is instructive here for the ways in which it parallels, from a social-identity standpoint, the implication of a former self as inadequate. Riley (1991: 280–281) proposes that as individuals our sense of identity is both informed by what others tell us 'all the time and in no uncertain way', and grounded in internal, linguistically-organised systems, acquired before we reach the age of five, that allow us to categorise people generally. A child's experience of a bilingual identity may be positive or negative depending, to a possibly substantial degree, on the respective status of his or her two languages. Thus, the bilingual individual experiences both gains and losses on the social level as well as psychically. Who we *think* we are linguistically, and how worthwhile we think we are, is for Riley determined by who others think we are. To add a psychoanalytic twist to Riley's social-theory perspective, I suggest that it is not only other people but also one's own unconscious – but nonetheless present – recollection of who we *used to be* that tells us what we are, and whether we are worthy or not.

3. Such a temporary 'paralysis', should it become more permanent, might gesture towards a new interpretation of Selinker's concept of *fossilised* language:

> linguistic items, rules and subsystems which speakers of a particular [native language] will tend to keep in their [interlanguage] relative to a particular [target language], no matter what the age of the learner or amount of explanation and instruction he receives in the [target language].' (Selinker, 1972: 215)

## Chapter 3

# Looking and Looking Again: Memoirs of Second Language Learning

*When I hear my voice, I just hate it ... It is not simply that my ears hate my mouth, or my mouth hates my eyes. The inner conflict inhabits my entire being. This makes me feel that my own 'self' is falling apart. Now I have two 'me's' inside myself. A 'me' with whom I am familiar and with whom I feel connected ... The other 'me' is a stranger.*
Zhou Wu
*Language, Consciousness and Personal Growth: An Autobiographic Study of a Second Language Learner*, 1993

*Words do not come from words.*
J.B. Pontalis
*Love of Beginnings*, 1993

### Searching for Stories

How can we contrive to make silence speak? For it is reticent: by its very nature it embodies no inclination to narrate itself. The story of silence, especially silence in language learning, has somehow to be coaxed out of its dwelling place and tricked into relating. Or – and here we come to another paradox – into a kind of *not*-relating: this project is, in fact, the search for a story not told, at least not told consciously, a story of what Phillips (1999: 42) has called the 'inarticulate self before language ... the passionate life without words'. To recast Phillips' assertion, that words are more than a substitute for wordlessness (1999: 43), in the context of silence within language is to propose that 'Words are not merely an explanation of silence; they are something else entirely'. The same can arguably be said for the spaces between the words: they are not just empty spaces. How, then, can we find a way to make words, and the spaces between them, tell the story of silence?

Psychoanalysis works at taking hints from silence, at listening to the unspoken. Madeleine Grumet's (1990: 322) reflection on autobiographical writing as 'both things: inner and outer, personal and public, spontaneous and considered, mind and body', reminds us that narratives about the self form a curious collecting place of experience, memory, desire, anxiety and interpretation, weaving together the present and the past, the recognised, the mis-recognised and the denied. Thus, while other research methodologies might offer significant insight into the phenomenon of silence in second language learning, for me the fit between psychoanalytic theory and narrative analysis seems to invite thinking about that phenomenon in ways that are not only of considerable interest but also potentially quite fruitful. At this point in my project I must do two things. I must find moments, within texts, in which the experience of silence in the interrelated processes of identity construction and second language acquisition is articulated accidentally, despite itself. I must also find ways to engage with other moments, in which silence is not actually articulated at all, but rather hints obliquely at itself, in texts that gesture towards questions of anxiety, conflict and ambivalence, and loss.

Silence may be one aspect of the process of second language acquisition that can be best known only after its passing, a component of the experience neither assimilated nor consciously perceived at the time it occurs but which might later be remembered, reworked and ultimately recounted. This peculiar process of experiencing and assimilating events, untimely yet perfectly timed, is one way of understanding the Freudian concept of *Nachträglichkeit* – deferred action – and correspondingly, the *nachträglich* usefulness of narration:

> It is not lived experience in general that undergoes a deferred revision but, specifically, whatever it has been impossible in the first instance to incorporate fully into a meaningful context. The traumatic event is the epitome of such unassimilated experience ... Deferred revision [*Nachträglichkeit*] is occasioned by events and situations, or by an organic maturation, which allow the subject to gain access to a new level of meaning and to rework his earlier experiences. (Laplanche & Pontalis, 1973: 112)

If a traumatic event can be accessed by the subject only after it has been reworked psychically and assimilated, narrative may prove a helpful methodology for holding events – a collecting place for all the anxieties, desires, memories and interpretations related to the events themselves – until the self is able to do the required working through. It may be particularly helpful when the events it contains are traumatic. My position is that within the context of silence in second language acquisition, the traumatic event that narrative holds and later interprets is the loss of the self that dwelled in the first language, along with the previous losses of the prior selves that informed that one. The first of these, according to Freud, is the lost connectedness with the mother, and the second, in Phillips' view, is the loss of the non-speaking, imagined-as-omnipotent self.

Still, to engage with narrative is a peculiar kind of work. Catherine Kohler Riessman (1993: 68) points out that there is no single way, no 'set of formal rules or standardised technical procedures' to analyse narrative, to interpret another's analysis of it, or even to validate either narrative or analysis. To begin with the obvious, researchers may apply any number of frameworks and methods to their analyses. Subsequently, different readers' social, intellectual and personal histories contribute differently to their readings of a piece of research. What is clear, however, is that 'narratives are interpretive and, in turn, require interpretation ... [and that our] analytic interpretations are partial, alternative truths ...' (Riessman, 1993: 22). What are the implications of working with 'partial, alternative truths' as a gesture in the direction of understanding silence in second language learning? How shall we answer when Riessman (1993: 64) asks, 'How are we to evaluate a narrative analysis? Can one tell a better one from a worse one?' For the assertion that narrative provides only partial, alternative truths begs two questions: part of what? alternative to what?

Riessman further argues that what can be said about narrative analyses can equally be said about narratives themselves. They are interpretive events; they change from one individual to the next and from moment to moment; they locate themselves within social and political discourses and are thus neither neutral nor objective. Psychoanalytic theory might add that narrative is also situated within, even as it emerges from, the individual self that creates it. And this self is but one edition of itself. Britzman and Pitt (2000: 5), in a discussion of the difficulties of narrating teaching and learning., remark that '[i]n psychoanalysis, as one narrates experience and retells events, the narratives perform the very conflicts at stake, but now as new editions, and so hold potential for constituting events as constructions'. In 'read[ing] narratives for the qualities of their dynamics rather than for the stability of their content', and working 'against the usual distinction that data and its analysis are discrete', Britzman and Pitt suggest that if, as for Riessman, the events recounted by a narration are in a sense always regarded from an interpretive distance, they are also always immediately present in a kind of persistent, and recursive, working through. If the truth of a narrative is in either of these ways partial or alternative, as Riessman would have it, it is no less true for that.

Further, on close examination the very partialness of a narrative might gesture towards what it leaves out, what it does not – because it cannot – express on its face. And silence, because of this very inexpressibility, may be precisely what is being hinted at: the story not told that nevertheless, and in spite of itself, offers itself up to a telling. Robert Coles (1989) recounts psychotherapeutic practices that encourage the relating of personal stories.

Leslie Bloom's (1998) *Under the Sign of Hope* similarly confronts the issue of silence within narrative itself: the importance of attending to the unspoken, to the part of the story that is not told. And Wendy Hollway and Tony Jefferson theorise the tendency of story 'to contain significances beyond the teller's intentions [as] what it shares with the psychoanalytic method of free associations' (Hollway & Jefferson, 2000: 35) – in other words, the power of narrative to allow the kinds of psychical interference with consciously-told stories that can be read psychoanalytically as marking the intrusion, into those stories, of the unconscious mind. Though their work is with interviews, Hollway and Jefferson's proposal for allowing such interference lends itself equally to the present study of written narrative since, for psychoanalysis, the greatest part of our psychical lives goes on without our knowing – consciously – about it. 'We may know what is on our minds, but not what is on the other minds inside us', reflects Phillips (1999: xx), and it is those other minds inside us that perform a great deal of the work of constructing our lives, whether verbally or in text. Roy Schafer concurs: 'experience is made or fashioned; it is not encountered, discovered, or observed, except upon secondary reflection', and even conscious 'introspection does not encounter ready-made material' (Schafer, 1992: 23). Taken together, the work of these theorists bolsters the view that psychoanalytic thought, SLA research and autobiographical writing can collaborate in the struggle to provide insight into, and to invite new kinds of thinking about, the individual, learning and the richness of silence. In a study of silence in language acquisition, particularly as a symptom of loss and conflict, such hints and invitations may be all that is offered. It may be that the closest we can come to the individual learner's language acquisition experience is to read the story of that experience. I move now to engage some of those stories.

Two subgenres of relevant narrative writing emerge from a search for the story of silence in second language learning. One category includes diaries and other similar accounts written by second-language learners with the express aim of recounting language acquisition experiences, often for use as a research tool. Their named purpose is to record the learner's subjective experience of what happens during the language learning process. Many of these have been examined closely by SLA research for clear evidence of environmental and social variables (Schumann & Schumann, 1977), and for explanations of numerous individual differences in language learning, including anxiety and competitiveness (Bailey, 1983) and affective response to instruction (Ellis, 1989). My engagement with them will take the form of a kind of psychoanalytic search for stories about silence, not explicitly told, but which nevertheless hint at conflict and ambivalence within learners. In particular, Bailey's 1983 article on 'Looking *at* and *through* the Diary Studies' (Bailey's emphasis), whose subtitle names its objective, also anticipates my own wish, which is to look *within* the diaries, beyond what they say at what they leave out, and into the spaces between the words where silence might dwell.

But I will return to the diaries in the next chapter. My immediate task is to explore another kind of narrative writing that bears on the question of silence in second language learning: namely autobiographical writing and memoir. In this writing, silence and the ambivalence, loss and conflict of which it is symptomatic seem at times to be quite consciously recalled, named, elaborated and interpreted on the part of the writer, whether or not silence is the stated topic of the text. More often, though, the memoirs and the diaries do no more than intimate either at silence or at the implications underlying it. And yet, although these accounts may make no overt mention of a silent period as such – indeed often *because* they do not – for reasons enumerated at the beginning of this chapter they both, in my view, lend themselves quite readily to a psychoanalytic inquiry.

Worth noting is that some second-language researchers have also examined this genre of writing, though with aims different from the present study. For example, John Schumann has assessed Hoffman's (1989) and Kaplan's (1993) memoirs for 'how their stimulus appraisals fuelled their language learning' (Schumann, 1997: 113). And it is further important to acknowledge that all the works engaged here have their origins in distinct socio-historical and linguistic contexts, and could certainly be organised and usefully studied with reference to those frameworks and the impacts they have on their authors. For this study, however, I have chosen to organise them psychoanalytically. My work is to look *inside* them, to take up the hints they might offer either through talking about, or through avoiding talking about, ambivalence and conflict, loss and anxiety, and the silence that might sometimes be their symptom. Still, although I am not undertaking an interpretation of the social and historical contexts of the memoirs and the diaries, either individually or in relation to one another, I cannot help but notice, even given the numerous differences between them, how a psychoanalytic interpretation of the individual narratives holds across, and even despite, those differences. And this finding, in turn, might later gesture towards the possibility of a psychoanalytic reading that moves back out from inside the narratives themselves and turns its gaze on the socio-historical discourses that inform them, and on the complex webs of relationships between and among discourses and narratives. But that is another project. For now, let us turn to the memoirs.

## Split by the Difference: Eva Hoffman

Eva Hoffman immigrated to Canada from Poland in 1959. Her 1989 memoir, *Lost in Translation: A Life in a New Language*, tells the story of that journey – of her sense at the time that leaving Poland meant being 'pried out of my childhood, my pleasures, my safety' (Hoffman, 1989: 4) and 'pushed out of the happy, safe enclosures of Eden' (1989: 5), and also of her later experience of learning to speak and, ultimately, to make a life in English. The language she uses is vivid in its description of the tensions at work in the space she occupies between the English and Polish languages, and between Canadian and Polish cultures. She tells us, 'The very places where language is at its most conventional ... are the places where I feel the prick of artifice' (1989: 106). And she goes on:

> But mostly, the problem is that the signifier has become severed from the signified ... 'River' in Polish was a vital sound, energized with the essence of riverhood, of my rivers, of my being immersed in rivers. 'River' in English is cold-a word without an aura. (Hoffman, 1989: 106)

For Hoffman, such a 'radical disjoining between word and thing is a desiccating alchemy, draining the world not only of significance but of its colors, striations, nuances – its very existence. It is the loss of a living connection' (1989: 107). In this passage Hoffman relates graphically, even painfully, the dissonance she experiences between the language and the world she has left behind and those she is learning. She is lost in a kind of 'no-place' between the two worlds, possessing fragments of both, but complete in neither, lacking Schutz's (1964: 95) 'trustworthy recipes for interpreting the social world'.

The idea that our understanding of words depends not only on our facility with a specific language but also on our identity as part of a social and cultural environment is taken up by Riley (1991: 279), who identifies language as 'the principal channel of sociocultural knowledge' and demonstrates how the knowledge of certain words is related to social iden-tity even in one's native tongue – no one knows every word in any language. But what Hoffman is talking about here seems to be something more elemental, more visceral: she knows the word, can think it, say it and write it, but cannot 'feel' its meaning.

Hoffman is not literally silent; outwardly she functions very well in her second language. But in terms of her self-expression – that is, the expression of her self – this period of her life is effectively voiceless. No stranger to the language of psychoanalysis, she describes how the 'worst losses come at night' when she waits for 'that spontaneous flow of inner language which used to be my night time talk with myself, my way of informing the ego where the id had been'. But, 'Nothing comes. Polish, in a short time, has atrophied ... [and in] English, words have not penetrated to those layers of my psyche from which a private conversation could proceed' (Hoffman, 1989: 107).

Hoffman's recollection of the loss of her bedtime self-talk also suggests that in her case the impact on her identity of the second language acquisition process is manifested as a disruption of her *inner* speech (Vygotsky, 1997). In addition, there are echoes in Hoffman's words of the shattered object-relationship discussed in the previous chapter in relation to first language acquisition. She has lost – perhaps not completely but to a very troubling degree – her ability to converse with herself, to connect different parts of her inner world with each other. This ability has disappeared, or been dramatically attenuated, like the imagined omnipotence of the unindividuated, pre-language infant. Later, Hoffman expresses even more passionately the sense of an identity lost, or alienated, or deprived of itself in the moment of suspension between languages. 'Linguistic dispossession', as she refers to it, 'is a sufficient motive for violence, for it is close to the dispossession of one's self. Blind rage, helpless rage is rage that has no words – rage that overwhelms one with its darkness' (Hoffman, 1989: 124).

For Hoffman, it seems, wordlessness is also a kind of blindness, a fog that covers the world. To be unable to voice her thoughts as fully in her second language as she can in her first, itself a kind of enforced partial silence, is also to have no vision, to see her new, second world and its inhabitants through a kind of

> verbal blur [that] covers these people's faces, their gestures with a sort of fog. I can't translate them into my mind's eye. The small event, instead of being added to the mosaic of consciousness and memory, falls through some black hole, and I fall with it. What has happened to me in this new world? I don't know. *I don't see what I've seen, don't comprehend what's in front of me. I'm not filled with language any more, and I have only a memory of fullness to anguish me with the knowledge that, in this dark and empty state, I don't really exist.* (Hoffman, 1989: 108; my italics)

What does it mean to be emptied of language, to have been dispossessed of one's first linguistic self and to have found, or made, no replacement? It seems that for Hoffman it means to disappear from her own internal world as well as from the world of others. Winnicott maintains that individuals need to feel authentically themselves in order to be emotionally healthy. His claim is that for human beings the inauthentic experience of feeling 'unreal, of feeling possessed, of feeling they are not themselves ... of being nothing, nowhere' (Winnicott, 1967: 33) is a symptom of denial of the self. Hoffman's memory of her sense of isolation, invisibility, and the loss of her linguistic connection with both the outside world and her inner self is expressed in language that also recalls the connection Phillips makes between words and bodies and, conversely, the disconnection from bodies that wordlessness brings. Stranded between two linguistic identities, Hoffman is metaphorically faceless, unseen and unseeing, unfelt and unfeeling. Of her body, which fails her need for self-expression just as language fails her, she writes:

> The mobility of my face comes from the mobility of the words coming to the surface and the feelings that drive them ... But now I can't feel how my face lights up from inside; I don't receive from others the reflected movement of its expressions, its living speech. People look past me as we speak. What do I look like, here? Imperceptible, I think; impalpable, neutral, faceless. (Hoffman, 1989: 147)

Hoffman further describes difficulties with language – difficulties with words themselves – in oddly revealing metaphors that acknowledge the incapacity of her physical and psychical being to tolerate the foreign body that is her new language. Moments of conventionality in language 'are the places where [she feels] the prick of artifice', and she manufactures a kind of psychical antibody to that artifice: 'There are some turns of phrase to which I develop strange allergies' (Hoffman, 1989: 106). Hoffman contrasts the English of her Polish acquaintances – 'jagged and thick' – with that of native English speakers whose speech embodies 'an easy flow and a plea-sure in giving words a fleshy fullness' (1989: 122). And the moment, many years after her introduction to her second language, when she finally cracks 'the last barrier between [herself] and the language – the barrier [she] sensed but couldn't get through', is recounted in physical, sensuously-oriented terms. She experiences 'tasting the sounds on the tongue, hearing the phrases somewhere between tongue and mind', when 'words become, as they were in childhood, beautiful things ... crosshatched with a complexity of meaning, with the sonorities of felt, sensuous thought' (1989: 186). In this moment, which recalls Freud's orally-framed concept of first judgement, Hoffman determines that her new language is something to take in, to feast on, rather than to spit out.

So what, precisely, is lost in translation? For Hoffman, meaning, at the very least: she knows that 'to translate a language, or a text, without changing its meaning, one would have to transport its audience as well' (Hoffman, 1989: 273). But more profoundly, in order to make 'a life in a new language' one has to 'make a shift in the innermost ways'. Hoffman writes,

'I have to translate myself' (1989: 211). And that translated self can never be remade precisely as it was before the translation, just as the self that possesses a first language is no longer the self of Phillips' (1999: 42) 'passionate life without words'.

Though Hoffman becomes able to make interest, work and love in the new language that 'has entered [her] body, has incorporated itself in the softest tissue of [her] being' (Hoffman, 1989: 245), echoes of her earlier Polish-language self persist. And in her recognition of these echoes I also read a remembering – of the self, albeit unnamed specifically, that lived prior to the first language, along with a continuing sense of mourning for that self. There is, Hoffman laments, 'no returning to the point of origin, no regaining of a childhood unity' (1989: 273). It seems as if the loss of unity – that is, of a unified self – that first took place in the translation from non-speaking to speaking self, is recalled in all subsequent translations. And 'the wholeness of childhood truths is intermingled with the divisiveness of adult doubt' (1989: 273).

Still, this intermingling is not all bad news. Hoffman finds that her psychotherapy, undertaken in English and not Polish, 'becomes ... a route back to that loss which for me is the model of all loss'. She tells us: '[I]n English, I wind my way back to my old, Polish melancholy. When I meet it, I re-enter myself, fold myself again in my own skin'. Again recalling Phillips, it appears that words – this time spoken in another tongue, in what Lacan would call an *other* tongue – are the route back into Hoffman's own body; living in two languages she finds that she 'can move between them without being split by the difference' (Hoffman, 1989: 274).

Split by the difference – in memoirs that recall movement from a first language to a second, the motif of splitting is a recurrent metaphor for conflict and ambivalence. Exactly what is being split varies, however. Individuals may experience splitting in different ways. For example, as a contributor to Diane Belcher and Ulla Connor's (2001) collection of *Reflections on Multiliterate Lives*, Anna Söter, a professor of English education highly successful in her second language, recalls the challenges she has nevertheless experienced, and continues to experience, writing in her second language. To illustrate how her 'native language [German] may ... have left a residual impact' (Söter, 2001: 73) on her thinking and on her academic writing in English, Söter remarks that at times, when trying to describe emotions, she must look to German to express herself accurately. She reflects: 'I do not believe we ever truly 'shed' our native tongue ... My occasional resorting to German for a thought must reflect an orientation that suggests English cannot work for me on those occasions' (Söter, 2001: 72). And she continues:

The reverse applied [at university] when writing my papers in German literature. Given that I had not 'thought' about German literature in German, I found myself turning to English and even made attempts to 'Germanicise' English words because they expressed a concept that I had only thought about in English. (Söter, 2001: 72)

It is important to note that Söter is here describing the writing process specifically, rather than the language-learning process in general. What is fascinating about her recollection, however, in addition to the way in which she calls on each of her first and second languages to facilitate the articulation of a different component of her inner world (either emotional or intellectual), is its implication that the inverse is also true. Certain aspects of her inner world seem to be effectively blocked from expression, at least to some degree, unless she 'resorts to' the appropriate language. In this her experience resonates with Hoffman's.

So does that of another contributor to Belcher and Connor's collection, social work professor María Juliá, whose first and second languages are Spanish and English respectively. In an interview with Diane Belcher, Juliá (2001: 181) elucidates some of the complexities inherent in relations between first and second languages. She relates that, despite her many years using English, and the fact that 'English is the only language that [she uses in her] life now', nevertheless it can still be 'hard to find the right words to express what you want to say in a second language' (2001: 183). The narratives of both Söter and Juliá suggest that, even in individuals who function extremely well (and even almost exclusively), in a second language, there may persist gaps between that language and the mother tongue and, I maintain, gaps between identities (or between different components of identity) as these relate to and are entwined with language.

In addition to different kinds of splitting as evinced by the writing difficulties of Söter and Juliá, splits or ruptures can occur within the same individual along multiple fault lines. And Hoffman (1989) is a case in point. For her, there is a split between signifier and signified – between words and the world they represent. There is another split rending apart her body and her language, or her lack of language: the sense of 'facelessness' that she experiences, referred to above, is not only metaphorical. And a third split, albeit eventually healed, is the one between the unified, felt, bodily integrated self of Hoffman's first language and the faceless, blinded, unhearing, skinless, empty, translated self that recalls, but cannot retell, its predecessor.

Hoffman further describes an intense experience of feeling lost – lost even to herself – in a kind of liminal space between languages and between cultures that is shaped by loss and conflict. Her silenced self-expression is one kind of silence; she is unable to 'speak herself', that is, to make *her self* heard or known even to herself. This loss of the capacity to articulate is new, and deeply troubling. But further, her self cannot speak its present incarnation to the world it now lives in, because it is not understood: 'I feel I'm not seen ... Imperceptible, I think; impalpable, neutral, faceless' (Hoffman, 1989: 147). The young Hoffman, disconnected from her earlier self because her first language cannot deliver her into the realm of the outside, and without sufficient English to make herself understood, has no public face, no public self. Here, then, is one more split – the public from the private, the outside from the inside – that recalls earlier ruptures and separations on the one hand, and earlier unities on the other. The fact of a private (first) and a public (second) language exacerbates this distinction. Profoundly difficult in Hoffman's case since, in addition to the difficulties of learning and making a life in a second language, she experiences the 'atrophy' of her first language, this division between the private and the public is a frequently-narrated aspect of the memoirs of second-language learners.

## Public and Private Selves: Richard Rodriguez

To the already-complex process of second language acquisition, Richard Rodriguez's (1988) autobiography, *Hunger of Memory,* adds the social and political dimensions of linguistic colonialism and racial/ethnic identity. Grumet's (1990: 322) articulation of autobiographical writing as embodying outer and inner, public and private components can be mapped onto Rodriguez's narrative, which speaks eloquently to a split, manifested in a silence like Hoffman's but even more utterly wordless, between public and private languages, and by extension between public and private selves.

First, Rodriguez describes himself as a child unusually aware of the differences between English and his native Spanish, happy at home but '[unsettled] to hear [his] parents struggle with English' (Rodriguez, 1988: 15). Second, he describes himself as a student, beginning his education 'able to understand some fifty stray English words' (1988: 11) and soon distinguishing 'English [as] intrinsically a public language [from] Spanish [as] an intrinsically private one' (1988: 20). Rodriguez loves his 'private' language, delights in it and, in a way that parallels Hoffman's (1989: 122) description of the 'fleshy fullness' of a native English speaker, he remembers that delight. He recalls the way 'tongues explored the edges of words, especially the fat vowels', 'the twirling roar of the Spanish *r*' and the pleasures of 'voices singing and sighing, rising, straining, then surging, teeming with pleasure that burst syllables into fragments of laughter'

(Rodriguez, 1988: 18). But what of the public language, English? Rodriguez simply does not speak it: 'I couldn't say. I wouldn't try to say ... Three months. Five. Half a year passed. Unsmiling, ever watchful, my teachers noted my silence' (1988: 20).

Surprisingly, considering its protractedness, but quite unremarkably if we remember the commonplace metaphors of silence as empty, insignificant, without substance and not worthy of notice, Rodriguez does not say a great deal about his silent period as such. What he does narrate is how it begins to come to an end after his worried teachers visit his home and instruct his mother and father to speak to him and his siblings in English. He recalls the moment of his parents' compliance with an explicit acknowledgement of the loss it incorporates:

> What would [my parents] not do for their children's well being? And how could they have questioned the Church's authority which those [teachers – Roman Catholic nuns] represented? In an instant, they agreed to give up the language (the sounds) that had revealed and accentuated our family's closeness. The moment after the visitors left, the change was observed. '*Ahora*, speak to us *en inglés*', my father and mother united to tell us. (Rodriguez, 1988: 21)

From a sociological perspective, this moment offers a clear and disturbing example of a pedagogically-driven manifestation of linguistic colonialism. In addition, however, and germane to the present discussion, as Rodriguez narrates it the moment is curiously resonant in its reiteration of the other losses, within and outside the second language acquisition process, which I have been exploring psychoanalytically. The family has until this moment been a unit. The language Rodriguez's parents agree to 'give up' is the one that has both created and expressed that unity. But in an instant the parents shift; says Rodriguez, *they* 'unite to tell *us*' – the children – how things must change. There is a split articulated here, a rift between the adults and the children in the family that takes the form (and is narrated in the language) of both a loss and a separation. The unit of the family has been ruptured; two new units have resulted from the break.

Another difference between this separation and the primary individuation process first theorised by Freud is that each new unit contains more than one member. Still, Rodriguez's language implicitly places the units in opposition to each other – *them* and *us*, the parents and the children, the (adult) other and the (child) self, the outside and the inside. Until that moment of separation through language, of the penetration by the public, outside world of the private, inner family circle, Spanish has constituted the private sounds of his home and family life, has 'transformed the knowledge of [his] public separateness and made it consoling – the reminder of intimacy' (Rodriguez, 1988: 18). All at once, that consolation, that reminder, is gone. English, previously just alien, becomes 'suddenly heartbreaking' when, or because, it is spoken by his parents. 'Those *gringo* sounds they uttered', recalls Rodriguez, 'startled me. Pushed me away' (1988: 21). The sounds push him away, and in a strange twist they also turn the 'insider' that Rodriguez had been within his family into an outsider. Linguistically, he is now 'outside' both at school, where his Spanish has never held purchase, and at home, where it used to, but does no longer. How reminiscent of the first traumatic individuation, when the child first perceives its mother as other to itself! Indeed, the echoes of that primary separation, for Rodriguez, may well have been loud in their own right, but they must surely have been made deafening by the fact that the separation was imposed on him by his parents at the insistence of his teachers.

Let us further recall Phillips' discussion of the losses that accompany the gains implicit in making a (first-language) speaking self out of a non-speaking one: 'the child is all the time giving things up – omnipotence, desire for and dominion over the parents, *babbling* – in order to secure the supposedly more viable satisfactions of maturity' (Phillips, 1999: 39). In the story of Richard Rodriguez we have a doubling of that relinquishment. For Rodriguez has already made his initial entry into the world of speech, gained the measure of autonomy that language brings, and left behind – or compromised – his inarticulate self and its accompanying fantasies of omnipotence. And now he must do it again, must once more '[leave] more than one home' (1999: 42), not, this time, out of the unmediated unity of pre-language silence but, in the sense articulated by Phillips, out of a self already reconciled to accommodation.

To the reader there seems to be a kind of dreadful trick, a betrayal, in the insistence of his parents and teachers on the abandonment of the family's private language. Oddly, however, Rodriguez's discussion of betrayal positions himself, quite explicitly, as its agent:

> For my part, I felt that I had somehow committed a sin of betrayal by learning English. But betrayal against whom? ... *I felt that I had betrayed my immediate family.* I *knew* that my parents had encouraged me to learn English. I *knew* that I had turned to English only with angry reluctance. But once I spoke English with ease, *I came to feel guilty. (This guilt defied logic.) I felt that I had shattered the intimate bond* that had once held the family close. (Rodriguez, 1988: 30; italics in original)

This passage does not 'defy' the logic of psychoanalytic theory at all. Interpreted psychoanalytically, it reads like a very predictable introjection. It speaks directly to Rodriguez's ambivalence, to the conflict between what he *knows* and what he *feels*, between his deep longing to move out into the world and his equally powerful desire to remain safely at home, physically, linguistically and psychically. His linguistic victory is hard won, for it also embodies a psychical defeat, its pleasures attenuated by the losses that accompany them. He is shattered. Like Hoffman before she found her home in both languages, he is 'split by the difference' – or rather by double differences: between his first- and second-language selves and their corresponding identities as, respectively, a member of a family unit and a worldly individual; and also between his conflicting desires to maintain those selves, each uniquely on one hand, and both together on the other.

But perhaps there are additional ways of considering these conflicting desires, other lenses through which they can be viewed. Linked to Phillips' assertion that learning to speak means giving up, or at least attenuating, an unspeaking self, is his recognition of the goal of maturity that seems to make the giving up worthwhile (Phillips, 1999: 39). Freud might articulate this goal of maturity as a part of the pleasure that accompanies and mitigates the unpleasure of relinquishing a former self. It may be helpful to speculate about potential implications of this psychical relationship between pleasure and unpleasure, between achieving a goal and giving something up in order to achieve it. In this specific context we might ask what rewards, other than the anticipation of engagement with speakers and the culture of the second language, might make giving up a first-language self worthwhile. Might being 'split by the difference' serve some other purpose?

One way of considering the notions of a division between public and private selves or between selves within and outside of the family, which Rodriguez's case exemplifies, is to examine them in the context of the psychical fantasy in which an individual's family is altered – a concept that Freud (1909) termed the *family romance*. In psychoanalytic theory, the family romance arises out of the child's awakening 'feeling of being slighted [because] ... he feels he is not receiving the whole of his parents' love and, most of all, [because] ... he feels regret at having to share it with brothers and sisters' (Freud, 1909: 237–38). It consists of an imagined replacement of the child's actual parents with others – often those who possess elevated social standing: a child may, for example, imagine that she was a foundling, or adopted at birth, and that her 'real' parents are royalty.

Rodriguez's story of ruptured relations between parents and children, which occurred when his mother and father, at the insistence of his teachers, made him speak English, is told in language that seems to contradict his self-blaming statement to the effect that it was Rodriguez himself who *'had shattered the intimate bond*' that had once held the family close' (Rodriguez, 1988: 30; italics in original). It seems that it is not he but rather his parents who, in their insistence that he speak English, have begun to produce the *'gringo* sounds ... that pushed [him] away' (1988: 21), breaking the close ties of family that their common language has previously reinforced. In this speculative scenario, the new language functions as a kind of tool that both facilitates and explains the child's separation, linguistically and otherwise, from the family. In turn, the fact of the linguistic separation furthers the fantasy of the family romance. The child has one more reason on which to base his unconscious wish to be more fully separate: to justify the fantasy that the family of which he is a part is not truly his. If we speculate that some form of family romance fantasy may be at play in Rodriguez's unconscious imagination, he is, by virtue of his parents' role in the linguistic division of the family, absolved of at least some of the guilt he might unconsciously experience about that fantasy. And this might be one of the rewards, one of the pleasures, of moving from one language to another and from one self to another, that help diminish the unpleasure that accompanies the loss or attenuation of the first-language identity. But because such pleasures can only diminish unpleasure, and cannot eradicate it, ambivalence and silence persist. Rodriguez might be able, in a sense, to use difference to initiate and justify the fantasy of a split, but he is also, like Hoffman, split *by* that same difference.

In addition to the conflicts explored above, which concern different editions of the self and different configurations of the relations between self and others, along with the wishes that inform and are informed by them and the conflicts that these wishes generate between them, there are other questions that invite engagement. I refer to questions about conflicts within what might be described, for the sake of clarity, as one particular edition of the self or, alternatively, as one particular moment in the constantly shifting and re-making self. More specifically, the kind of conflict to which I now turn is one articulated by Winnicott (1965) and subsequently taken up by Pitt (2000): a conflict between the individual's wish to hide the self and the desire to communicate it.

## The Secret Self: Patrick Chamoiseau

For Winnicott (1965: 179), 'the right not to communicate' is grounded in what Pitt (2000: 65) terms his 'insistence that there exists, at the very core of the individual, a permanently isolated and secret self'. The argument that

Pitt advances is twofold. First, this secret self is in perpetual conflict with the individual's opposing needs to be known and to communicate. Second, by recognising this conflict we might begin to develop ways of thinking about why 'we experience telling (or showing) the details of our personal lives, not as illuminating the self for another, but as a threat to the integrity of the self' (2000: 67). Let us follow that argument to take a look at the implications it entails regarding conflict in second language learning and silence as a symptom or manifestation of it.

There is something intuitively appealing about Winnicott's idea of a secret and private self. As Pitt suggests, however, it may present a problem for the discourse of object-relations theory, within which Winnicott himself worked and which privileges relationships between the self and other(s), beginning with the mother, in the creation and ongoing re-creation of personal identity. Still, this difficulty is not insurmountable, even if one accepts as a given the postulate that identity is made in relation to others, a tenet not only of object-relations theory but of other social-identity theories, such as those of Mead, Burkitt and Harré discussed in previous chapters.

It is reasonable to propose the existence, within the nascent human organism, of some primary feature, quality or energy – something that initiates the making of such inside/outside relations or, if one understands relationality as engaged from without, that enables the organism to respond to the overtures made towards it. Indeed, it is counter-intuitive to claim that relations can be made from nothing. Even the Freudian process of psychical separation from the mother, which the infant undergoes as it becomes aware of boundaries between itself and the world, requires the presence of something, some entity, that has the potential to become aware and to separate. Perhaps one way of thinking of this *something* is as a kind of psychical nucleus of being, out of which the self, in all its continually changing and re-changing versions, originates, and of which, significantly, a vestige always remains.

This sounds a little familiar, and it is. It resounds with Phillips' (1999) idea of the pre-language self, lost in a sense with the acquisition of language yet never totally relinquished, and present as a kind of shadow in every speech act, the inarticulate contribution of the unconscious to the relations we make with the world outside ourselves, through speech. In her paper, Pitt (2000: 65) prompts us to think about 'the notion that the most secret aspect of ourselves resides in the unconscious'. If the Winnicottian secret self is located topographically in the unconscious and chronologically at the beginning of identity formation, it must presumably also precede language within the individual, and thereby be vulnerable to the same disruption that the acquisition of language brings to the pre-language self (of which the secret self is, obviously, a part). To the extent, then, that the acquisition of language disturbs the pre-language self, it also challenges the secret self – inviting it to communicate, but threatening it with exploitation if the invitation is accepted. And therein lies a conflict. For pushing against each other are two desires: to keep the secret of the secret self, and to tell it.

To complicate matters further, language is more than a disruption to the unconscious secret self, and likewise more than a reminder of previous disruptions. It is also the very means by which the secret self can communicate itself, should it wish or be compelled to do so. What Pitt (2000: 65) calls 'something of a protest that can trail the pleasures of communication' is in part the ambivalence about whether to communicate the silent self or not. It is also the unconscious memory of the loss – of the non-communicating, inarticulate self – that accompanied or was implicated by the first decision to communicate, to open the mouth and let language in *to* the self, and let the self out through language. The secret self has a choice, but it is not an easy one.

The problem of choice bears directly on the issue of conflict in language learning, and in particular on silence as the symptom or manifestation of that conflict. If we do possess a secret self that can only be made known to others if access to it is granted, ambivalence regarding that access (or outright resistance to it) might well be demonstrated by silence. But within the process of second language acquisition, the invitation, or threat, made by language towards the secret self can be even more complex. As I have suggested, there are ways in which the process of second language acquisition can be mapped onto L1 acquisition in terms of psychical effect. Each process interferes with and changes, but does not fully destroy, the self that preceded it, and that interference is unconsciously experienced as a loss. With the concept of the secret self added to the second language acquisition mix, there are theoretically two languages through which the secret self could simultaneously choose to reveal or conceal itself, but the L2 offers the secret self the same two-sided coin of promise and threat as the L1: you can make yourself known, but you might wish you hadn't. And so the secret self is torn as it was with the first language between, as Phillips would have it, the gain and the loss: the promise of connection offered by self-revelation and the threat of lost privacy that must be defended against.

The already-tricky ambivalence of the secret self is rendered more problematic still in the case of an L2 learner, especially one like Hoffman who does not feel at home in either language, or one like Rodriguez who distinguishes the private from the public linguistically. For even if the self's wish to reveal itself should prevail despite its ambivalence, the individual, and the secret part of his or her self, is stuck between languages. The new language is not sufficiently acquired, and the old language is no longer adequate; the secret self, at this liminal moment, cannot be expressed even if the wish for expression is present. The faculty of language, the methodology for self-expression that originally bestowed the power to choose on the secret self, on the individual himself or herself, now takes that power away. It is another insult, another interference, another trick. The secret self, which in giving up its inarticulate edition acquired both the advantageous potential for expression and the troubling possibility of ambivalence, cannot now, in this moment between languages, maintain either expressibility or ambivalence; it must, at least temporarily, choose against communication. And the self, required by what Lacan names a 'forced choice' (Fink, 1996: 77) to submit to language in order not to be silenced by the linguistic Other, finds that its liminal location – between two languages and therefore outside both – has generated a new kind of forced-choice: silence.

How can the second-language-learning self tolerate the disappearance of the choice to communicate, and even of the possibility of resisting choice, of remaining ambivalent? With the door to expressibility in the first language closed behind her, and confronted with a not-quite-open door in the second lnguage, she must simply do the best she can. For Phillips, making good our losses is exactly what we do, in language and in life:

> We are born in turbulent love with the world, which is assumed to be made for us, of a piece with our wishes; then we suffer the humiliation of disillusionment, in which our rage is the last vestige of our hope. And then, if we are lucky ... we accommodate to our insufficiencies. We become the heroes and heroines of our own limitations: masters of absence. And if we are exceptional, we become wise, serene in our enlightened adaptation to the way the world is. (Phillips, 1999: 39–40)

Read as a piece of advice to the second-language learner, this passage hints at what 'the best we can do' might mean for an individual caught between languages: accommodation to insufficiencies, making do with the choices we have. One such choice seems to be to maintain speech while simultaneously silencing or repressing affect. While such a silence is not categorical – it does not show up as months and months without talk – it is nevertheless real. Hoffman (1989: 124) notices it in the 'rage that has no words' and in the rupture of words from what they signify: the word for river that in Polish seemed rich with meaning but that in English is 'a word without an aura' (Hoffman, 1989: 106). Rodriguez lives it too, in the contrast between home life, with its intimate familial pleasures, and life at school, where 'the instruction bids him to trust lonely reason primarily' (Rodriguez, 1988: 46).

There are other ways in which affect and its expression may be silenced, though speech goes on: ways not always as obvious as those articulated by Rodriguez and Hoffman, in which the forced choice not to communicate may be manifested. Patrick Chamoiseau, in another memoir of education and language, entitled *School Days* (Chamoiseau, 1997; translated from the French *Chemin d'École*), recounts his experience as a young boy in Martinique, and in so doing tells the story of another kind of silence. A victim of linguistic colonialism reminiscent of that which Richard Rodriguez experienced, at school Chamoiseau is forced to replace his Créole 'mama-tongue' with French, and in addition is subjected to malevolent teaching. He cannot express himself in French for linguistic reasons, and fear of his teacher prevents him from speaking in Créole. But fear of his mother's disapproval will not allow him to reveal himself at home either. In one especially moving passage, Chamoiseau, referring to himself as 'the little boy', describes how he begins to accommodate to the insufficiencies of his school life, transforming himself, as Phillips asserts we all do, into the hero of his own limitations and the master of his own absence in order to conceal his feelings about school from his mother:

> How his heart leapt to see her! ... And yet, areas inaccessible to Mam Ninotte [his mother] were piling up inside him. He'd begun hiding from her all his unavowable fears, his ignominious anxieties, those sorrows unlikely to earn him an extra dollop of affection. He kept his failures secret ... Grumbling about school to her would have released a flash flood of disapproval. So the little boy's mind began to focus on the idea of surviving the hardships of school. Surviving. Getting through it. And that, he could tell, was estranging him from his family by opening pockets of solitude in the core of his being. In order to keep his new secrets, he cast off subtle ties to the world and made himself opaque to Mam Ninotte. (Chamoiseau, 1997: 74)

In this memoir, written from the perspective of 'the little boy' who has, by the time of writing, grown to manhood, Chamoiseau-the-writer clearly interprets those new secrets that Chamoiseau-the-child hid from his mother as more than mere grumbling about school. He later describes himself as 'a walking secret' (Chamoiseau, 1997: 130) who tells his mother nothing at all, presenting his home life with a self as attenuated as the one he presents at school. Chamoiseau's little-boy self significantly resembles both Rodriguez and Hoffman as children, their lives and their identities split by conflict between home and school, between the public self and the private self, the intellect and the affect, the outside and the inside, the second language and the first.

Winnicott introduces another kind of split that has implications for silence in second language learning: the separation of the intellect from the whole individual. In the previous chapter I referred to Winnicott's essays, *Sum, I am* (1963a) and *Cure* (1970), as they detail his ideas about the development of the individual's understanding that she is a being separate from others. To be accomplished adequately, this process, enacted as the child's dependence on those around her decreases, requires what Winnicott (1970: 119) has called 'good-enough mothering and environmental provision of the holding variety'. He offers the example of a baby who cries when hungry; if the feeding is too long in coming, the infant loses the connection between the feeling of hunger and the satisfaction of being fed. This, for Winnicott, is a function of the child's intellect, and varies inversely with it. Thus a baby who has a greater intellectual capacity will be able to use such sensory clues as the sound of the caregiver's voice, the feeling of being picked up, the milky smell of the mother, to understand, earlier on relative to another child, that food is on its way. For Winnicott (1963a, 59) this is how 'the intellect helps in the tolerance of frustration'. And it can be put to useful purpose; it is one of the opportunities that caregivers have to begin to free themselves, gradually, from a baby's dependence.

However, Winnicott advances the view that, in the case of an infant endowed with

> an intellectual equipment that is well above average, the baby and the mother may collude in exploitation of the intellect which becomes split off – split off, that is from the psyche of psychosomatic existence and living ... [T]he baby begins to develop a false self in terms of a life in the split-off mind, the true self being psychosomatic, hidden and perhaps lost ... (Winnicott, 1963a: 59)

The split-off intellect, 'at its extreme, and in a person with a rich intellectual endowment ... can function brilliantly without much reference to the human being' (Winnicott, 1963a: 60). In other words, such a person, for whom the world cannot be relied on as a place of emotional safety, psychically separates mind from body and lives in her or his mind, valuing mind over the body, and thinking over feeling, because feeling is simply too dangerous.

I find meaningful connections between Winnicott's concept of the split-off intellect and the work of language. Language is an event of the mind, an intellectual activity. In its production, however, it is also a bodily function, and in its expressive and representational power it is a manifestation of emotional life as well. How might we imagine the implications for language, then, if an individual's intellect is, in a Winnicottian sense, separated from the rest of her self? Could the intellect, disconnected from affect, lose its power to represent and express the non-intellectual, split-off or sublimated aspects of the self? Or, alternatively, might it simply have nothing to say about the parts it can no longer access? Could silence be a consequence of this? And consider, conversely, a situation in which the emotive and affective aspects of a language are not yet known – a situation exemplified by that of the beginning second-language learner who cannot yet express emotions in the target language, including, to be sure, emotions about that language itself and her place in it. Might such a situation exacerbate, or even generate, such a split?

Winnicott does not speak directly to issues of first- or second-language acquisition. Still, it is a reasonable extension of his concept of the split-off intellect to consider the possibility that the kinds of language-learning experience described here might sometimes also be stories of a profound rupture in identity. Resonating with Hoffman's clearly-articulated recollection of feeling linguistically and therefore essentially, existentially, dispossessed is the experience of the young child described in the introduction to this study, who felt 'like nothing' when her teacher criticised her speech. Likewise, Zhou Wu, whose doctoral dissertation (Wu, 1993) recounts his experience of migrating to Canada from China in 1989, summarises in a few words (quoted as the epigraph to this chapter) what he perceives to be the disintegration of his identity as he realises that his English, which seemed perfectly adequate in China, is quite unsatisfactory in a Canadian context. If, for the individual whose intellect is split off from the self as a whole, it is the case that the world cannot be trusted, perhaps the body, as the source of dangerous feeling, cannot be trusted either. After all, the body in such a scenario is, in effect, part of the world that includes everything other than the intellect. And speaking involves both mind and body. Speaking a second language, speaking *in* a different tongue, is also in a sense speaking *with* a different tongue – using the tongue in different, difficult ways. Thus, the tongue is at once a tool of the mind and a part of the body. For the second-language learner, then, might it be possible that holding the tongue – remaining silent either literally or metaphorically – is a way of living in the mind when the world she is in, a new world, cannot be trusted?

## Mastering the Subject: Alice Kaplan

Alternatively, what if it is the world of the first-language self that cannot be trusted? The narratives I have explored have primarily concerned themselves with individuals' desires and difficulties in relation to acquiring a second language while maintaining – and feeling close ties with – a first. Might it also be the case that the wish of some learners is to erase that first language and the self it expresses, which also lives within it? It seems a strange question to raise in a study focusing on second language acquisition, but I raise it nevertheless, in order to lend further force to my position. I wonder, for example, about individuals who have fled oppressive conditions they may want to forget, or who, for whatever reason, wish to avoid being identified with a certain linguistic group. Might there be a way to experience second language learning that differs from the cruel denial of one's first language and culture, as experienced by Chamoiseau and Rodriguez, and from the 'loss' of self in the translation from one language to another, as recalled and told by Hoffman? Might the process of acquiring a new language mean, for some individuals, an escape rather than a prison? And what might be the nature of silence within that process? Might it mean something qualitatively different from the silences already explored?

A case in point – Alice Kaplan, in her memoir *French Lessons* (Kaplan, 1993), relates her experience of an obsessive need to excel in her second language because of the premature death of her father. Grappling with this deeply felt personal loss, Kaplan begins to lose interest in learning and is sent for a year to a Swiss boarding school. Later she writes that at the end of that year she 'had learned a whole new language (French) at boarding school but it was a language for covering pain, not expressing it' (Kaplan, 1993: 58). Fleeing an oppression that is not political but rather psychical, Kaplan's intellectual life takes over in a Winnicottian kind of splitting-off. Her feeling self cannot tolerate the unreliable, unspeakable world of loss and trauma, and so she finds a language in which the unspeakable does not have to be tolerated.

Many years later, writing her memoir, Kaplan recognises the profound interconnection between her language and her identity, connecting her obsession with French with the trauma of losing her father – 'French made me absent the way he was absent' (Kaplan, 1993: 203) – and describing it as a need for the 'quiet mastery of a subject' (1993: 55). This beautifully ambiguous phrase is peculiarly telling. During that year in Switzerland, Kaplan recounts, she becomes anorexic in her desperate need to master her physical self, while her proficiency in French not only allows her to 'master' her own subjectivity as well as the language, but also gives her the linguistic hiding place she deeply longs for. From then on, Kaplan's life in English is attenuated; she begins to make a life in French.

As an adult, she becomes a professor of French. Living in Paris Kaplan (1993: 209) feels 'at peace, [no-longer] split in two'. But still she asks: 'Why have I chosen to live in not-quite-my-own-language, in exile from myself, for so many years – why have I gone through school with a gag on, do I like not really being able to express myself?' (1993: 210) And she begins to answer her own question: 'I know now that my passion for French helped

me to put off what I needed to say, in English, to the people around me ...
Why did I hide in French? If life got too messy, I could take off into my
second world' (1993: 214–16) – her second world, her second self.

'Talking cures', writes Kaplan (1993: 130) ambiguously. The origin of this
phrase is attributed to Anna O., a patient of Freud and his collaborator
Breuer, who demanded that her therapy take place in English, rather than
in her native German (Kaplan, 1993: 130). This part of Kaplan's memoir is a
discussion of teacher–student relations – 'battles of the will with fierce
parental overtones' (1993: 120) – and the history of language teaching
methods. But Kaplan also uses the phrase 'talking cures' as an affirmative
statement: Anna O. is another Kaplan, cured of what ailed her by the help of
another language. For talking *does* cure. And speaking French, along with
reading and writing it, is what cures Kaplan. It effects this cure by giving
her a place to function linguistically where she does not have to acknowledge or reveal her deepest, unspeakable self, a revelation that would for her
be intolerable. What is more, in a sense suggestive of a kind of family
romance fantasy (Freud, 1909) born out of trauma, and resembling to a
degree that discussed with regard to Richard Rodriguez, she can use that
linguistic separateness as a tool to create and maintain distance. For it is
distance that she needs: between herself on the one hand and her father,
and the trauma caused by his death, on the other. And her life in French
gives her that distance. There, in her second language, she can work and
live until she is able to re-unite the split-apart aspects of herself.

Neither *French Lessons* nor the other memoirs I have referred to is
specifically a disquisition on silence in second language learning. They
only hint at it. But, as I have said earlier, hints may be all we have about
something as difficult to represent as silence. I have chosen Kaplan's
narrative because of the way it illuminates some of the powerful ways in
which language works as a methodology, not only for communicating the
self, but also for resisting communication. In Kaplan's memoir, unlike those
of Hoffman and Rodriguez, disappearing into a 'second world' is a way of
maintaining the control she needed over her 'first' world. But, for all three,
the sense of having two linguistic selves is similar. And the experiences of all
three speak to Britzman's (1998: 23) view of identity as 'an imaginary state of
perpetual emergency' – another ambiguous expression that depicts perfectly
the self as a site of both continual crisis and metamorphosing chrysalis.

Kaplan is not the only one who is troubled as well as healed by language.
The other authors examined in this section all offer evidence, through their
writing, that 'talking cures' (and also that writing cures). Aspects of their
writing also convey the sense that *not* talking is at times part of a talking
cure: that and finding, or making, a way to talk. Hoffman eventually finds

herself 'cured of the space sickness of transcendence' and, in understanding her own impermanence she finds 'a tenderness for everything that is always to be lost' (Hoffman, 1989: 274). Similarly, Rodriguez and Chamoiseau find that part of the work of healing the splits between their first and second languages, and the selves that live in those first and second languages, lies in telling their stories. Rodriguez, towards the end of his autobiography (1988: 176), tells us, 'I sit here in silence writing this small volume of words, and it seems to me the most public thing I have ever done ... I am making my personal life public'. And Chamoiseau (1997: 144) finishes his memoir with a poignantly lovely image of 'the little black boy bent over his notebook ... tracing, without fully realising it, an inky lifeline of survival'.

Before leaving this examination of the memoirs of second-language learners, it seems worthwhile to make two final comments. First, I reiterate the observation made at the beginning of this chapter, regarding the distinct socio-historical contexts out of which arose the specific experiences of those whose memoirs I have examined, from the racism and linguistic colonialism endured by Chamoiseau and Rodriguez to Kaplan's fiercely self-determined study of French. While those varying contexts are clearly significant, and undoubtedly deserving of their own enquiry, such an enquiry would be beyond the scope of this piece of work. What is significant for my study – and indeed what may gesture towards a psychoanalytic investigation of those contexts – are the ways in which silence, as a meaningful and even necessary part of the language acquisition process, seems to span the contextualisations themselves.

Second, from the perspective of SLA research, the writers whose memoirs are engaged in this chapter have their own motivations, unique and yet similar, for undertaking the second language learning process. Gardner and Lambert distinguish between:

> [at] one extreme an integratively oriented learner who in considering the learning task is oriented principally towards representatives of a novel and interesting ethnolinguistic community, people with whom he would like to develop personal ties ... [and at] the other extreme the instrumentally oriented language learner [who] is interested mainly in using the cultural group and their language as an instrument of personal satisfaction, with few signs of an interest in the other people per se. (Gardner & Lambert, 1972: 14–15)

Larsen-Freeman and Long follow Gardner and Lambert in describing integrative motivation as marked by the learner's wish 'to identify with another ethnolinguistic group' and in describing instrumental motivation as that 'in which the learner is motivated to learn a second language for utilitarian purposes, such as furthering a career, improving social status or meeting an educational requirement' (Larsen-Freeman & Long, 1991: 173). But the concept of motivation is not an entirely straightforward one: the binary distinction between the integrative and the instrumental is blurred. Ema Ushioda's (1996) work on the role of motivation in the area of learner autonomy (a concept that I elaborate in Chapter 5) complicates the binary by suggesting that learner motivation is

> shaped by the subjective value the individual attaches to the goals and incentives that operate in the learning context ... [and that individuals] vary considerably in the subjective value they ascribe to particular goals. (Ushioda, 1996: 16–17)

Even Gardner and Lambert (1972: 14–15) seem to imply, in speaking of instrumentally and integratively motivated learners as two 'extremes', that something must lie between those two extremes. And certainly, neither this nor the later characterisation of these two types of motivation (Larsen-Freeman & Long, 1991) refuses the possibility of a combination of both types being active in a particular learner. For me it is rather difficult to imagine motivation as purely of one sort or the other. Still, of the learners whose narratives are examined here, Eva Hoffman's motivation is arguably the most purely integrative. She wants, and needs, to immerse herself in her target language so as to be able to learn, and live in, a new country and a new culture. Even so, there are elements of instrumental motivation in her learning as well, and the experiences of Richard Rodriguez and Patrick Chamoiseau likewise seem to embody the two kinds of motivation. Alice Kaplan's motivation maps less directly onto the integrative-instrumental paradigm – and yet, although her aim was to learn French in order to escape, in a sense, from her English self, integrative and instrumental motivation both seem to be implicit to some degree in her experience.

It seems reasonable, almost intuitive, to conjecture that second-language learners whose goals are primarily instrumental might experience second language acquisition as a less difficult, less traumatic process in terms of psychical aspects. It also seems, albeit arguably, that the motivations of the language-learner diarists whose work I consider next are more instrumental than integrative, in that their goals are relatively 'clearly-defined and classifiable' (Ushioda, 1996: 17). And yet, as the following chapter will demonstrate, the diaries, and specifically moments of silence within the diaries, can be read psychoanalytically as embodying psychical difficulties strikingly similar to those in the autobiographical narratives already explored. I turn now to those diaries.

## Chapter 4

# Reading Between the Lines: Language Learner Diaries

*Whereof one cannot speak, thereof one must be silent.*
Ludwig Wittgenstein
*Tractatus Logico-Philosophicus*, Section 7, 1921

*I do not know,*
*I cannot say –*
*I would not tell you anyway.*
Schoolyard rhyme

### Why Diaries?

The concepts of 'the doubting game' and 'the believing game', originally developed by Peter Elbow (1973) as analytical methods for literary criticism and later applied by Larsen-Freeman (1983) to theories of second language acquisition, are reviewed once more by Kathleen Bailey (1991), with respect to her diary studies. Fundamentally, the doubting game 'emphasises objectivity – the separation of self (the subject) from the object under investigation' and 'takes a critical, questioning stance toward evidence and conclusions drawn from the data'. The believing game 'emphasises [that] a model of knowing as an act of constructing, an act of investment, an act of involvement' is 'an act of self-insertion, self-involve-ment – an act of projection' and 'is built on the idea that the self cannot be removed: complete objectivity is impossible' (Elbow, 1973: 148–49, 172–73).

Resonant with Grumet's (1990) writing about the usefulness of narrative research as a counterpoint to quantitative studies is Bailey's (1991: 65) assertion regarding both the possibility and the value of first-person narra-tive as a tool in SLA research. In the diary-study method, 'the subject becomes the object: we conduct (and read) diary studies to understand language learning as seen by the learners'. Bailey argues persuasively for the use of personal writing as a tool for research into language learning:

I would argue that the diary studies are absolutely essential to advancing our understanding of classroom language learning. At the present time we are working with an unrefined tool to craft an only dimly understood representation of language learning. Properly done, the diary studies can provide us with important missing pieces in this incredibly complex mosaic – pieces that may not be fully accessible by any other means. (Bailey, 1991: 87)

Part of the reason for Bailey's argument is the intrinsic complexity of the affective factors she is attempting to understand. This complexity is likewise implicated in two relationships: the first is between affective factors and the learner's success, or lack of success, at acquiring the target language, and the second is between affect and the researcher's interpretation of it. Supported by J. Oller's (1979) research on affective variables in language learning, Bailey contends that, because affect is often experienced by individuals internally rather than overtly manifested, researchers' conclusions are often the result of inferences, predictions and judgements about their subjects' motivations and feelings. In other words, the nature of affect in second language acquisition compels its investigation to be both speculative and interpretive. Despite that, it is no less significant an area of study, its central question for Bailey being, 'How can a researcher discover what individual students really do and think and feel during the language lesson?' (Bailey, 1983: 70–71)

I think this question ought to be preceded by another: *Can* a researcher discover what students do and think and feel? Perhaps this cannot be answered with a resounding affirmative; perhaps 'maybe' or 'partly' is the best we can hope for. That is, 'what individual students really do and think and feel' when they are learning a second language may be partly accessible through observation, and partly through reading and interpreting diaries written by these learners, and also partly, as explored in the previous chapter, through their memoirs and autobiographies. And I believe, with Bailey, that the effort is not only a worthwhile one, it is also crucial. At the same time, however, if we acknowledge that the self embodies aspects that are unconscious and not always, indeed only rarely, accessible to the conscious self, we must also admit that these discourses, even taken together, can only ever paint a partial picture. Still, perhaps they can be augmented: given its interest in the unconscious and the latent, the kind of informed speculation that psychoanalytic theory can provide may be helpful in this regard. While I acknowledge that the study of affect in general is a speculative art, and that the study of silence – viewed, as it often is, as an absence – is more speculative still, for me it is also the case that along with the 'important missing pieces in [the] incredibly complex mosaic' of language learning that learner diaries provide (Bailey, 1991: 87), they also yield up some of the richness of the silent spaces between those pieces.

Recognising and valuing the involvement of the self as at once subject and object of study is what Linda Brodkey (1996) seems to invite in her elaboration of a view of the validity of first person narrative, and subjective experience, as tools for learning. Working with the ambiguous word *bias*, she uses her mother's work of sewing, and within that work her mother's and her own recognition of 'how much depends on the bias' (Brodkey, 1996: 44), as a way of thinking about her personal educational experience, specifically the work of writing within that experience. Brodkey argues in favour of 'writing on the bias or not at all' (1996: 46), disputing, in a way consistent with Oller (1979) and Bailey (1983), the commonly-held but fallacious perception that 'third-person statements are unbiased (objective) and those in the first person are biased (subjective)' (1996: 45). Brodkey further asserts that:

[f]ar from guaranteeing objectivity, third person assertions too often record an unexamined routine in which the writers who follow a bias provided by, say, the 'objectivism' of journalism or science confound that worldview-theory-ideology with reality. The bias we should rightly disparage is that which feigns objectivity by dressing up its reasons in seemingly unassailable logic and palming off its interest as disinterest – in order to silence arguments from other quarters. (Brodkey, 1996: 46)

Here Brodkey is speaking of the form that writing takes, but her claim is also an implicit warning against the danger of regarding any worthwhile intellectual practice as entirely objective. 'Writing', she states, 'is about following a bias that cuts against the grain because, like sewing, writing recognises the third dimension of seemingly two-dimensional material' (Brodkey, 1996: 46).

Playing the believing game – by recognising the involvement of the self, the personal bias, in personal narrative – adds richness and possibility to the work of understanding that narrative, just as finding and cutting a piece of fabric on the bias enhances a finished garment. For Brodkey, personal narrative of the kind termed *autoethnography* (which includes not only her own story of learning to write but also, in the present discussion, the kinds of reflections found in the language-learner diaries' accounts of learning a new language) is 'a story told by the persistence of memory, which is selective, to be sure, [but] none the less instructive for that' (Brodkey, 1996: 27).

In this chapter, I engage in a believing game of my own, but with a twist. For, in addition to the stories told by the diarists and by those who interpret them, I believe that there are other stories that they are not telling. Further, I believe that they are not telling them because they are unable to tell them, because they do not, and indeed cannot, know what they are. These are the spaces between the pieces in Bailey's metaphorical mosaic (1991: 87). Psychoanalytic theory, with its insistence on the unconscious as the 'third dimension' of the individual that weaves invisible but persistent patterns into the fabric of existence (including that represented in narrative) offers assistance in the form of hints, which may be useful for reading diaries, as well as the interpretations of diaries that take the form of 'diary studies'. Thus my reading of this work, undertaken in acknowledgement of its speculative nature, aims to think about the hidden, silent stories that lie behind the told stories of second language learning, learning – and difficulties with learning – *not* consciously experienced by the learners.

As I mentioned in Chapter 3, the diaries considered in this chapter were written with the specific purpose of recording second language learning experiences, and used as research tools in the investigation of individual differences and other factors. This is an additional reason for their useful- ness since, as records of second-language-learning experiences in contexts that are often formalised, they add a more specifically pedagogical element to the exploration of silence in the second language acquisition process. Still, unsurprisingly in the light of their aims, silence is not their explicit focus. My work with them, as with the memoirs studied in the previous chapter, takes what Phillips (1999: 75) has called 'a stab at hinting' which, 'like a dream, tantalises us with the problem of interpretation, of what it would be like to get it right'. My desire to get both the hints and the inter- pretation right – to have the last word – is tempered by Phillips' reminder that 'there could be nothing more absurd than to have the last word on hint- ing'. Still, let us see, once more, where taking hints takes us.

## Reading and Interpreting the Diaries

Francine Schumann and John Schumann discuss the use of diary studies as a methodology for conducting 'in-depth longitudinal case studies exam- ining the social-psychological variables in SLL (second language learning) by individuals' (Schumann & Schumann, 1977: 241). Though they recog- nise the importance of cross-sectional studies in measuring some of the variables that affect language learning, their work aims to address the fact that such studies may not account for 'how various social-psychological factors affect an individual's perception of his own progress' (1977: 242). They point out that, in addition to the Western model of experimental psychology, there are other, traditionally Eastern, epistemologies that value self-observation as a way of acquiring understanding about events and processes, and go on to describe their undertaking to keep journals during periods of residency and language learning in Tunisia and Iran. Schumann and Schumann recorded

> daily events and the thoughts and feelings related to them in a log-like fashion, paying particular attention to cross-cultural adjustments and efforts made and avoided in learning the TL [target language] both in and out of class. (Schumann & Schumann, 1977: 243)

Their article presents their interpretations of those journals. As Schumann and Schumann acknowledge, however, journals are essentially private documents, and since they are not presented in their entirety in the article, I have no access to them. I draw, however, on Brodkey's (1996: 27) notion of narrative as a 'story told by the persistence of memory' that can be instructive despite its selectiveness, and on Britzman and Pitt's (2000: 5) claims with regard to the enmeshment of data and interpretation to assert the helpfulness of examining the interpretations: every interpretation is also, itself, a narration.

In terms of both language learning and affect, which she generalises as 'contentment' (Schumann & Schumann, 1977: 243), Francine Schumann draws a clear distinction between her time in Tunisia and her time in Iran. About her experience in Tunisia, she writes, 'I felt alienated from and hostile towards my environment, and these emotions usurped my energies such that I rarely could direct any to studying Arabic the entire time we lived there' (1977: 244). She attributes this alienation to generally uncomfortable living conditions that conflicted with her requirement for what she refers to as nest-building:

> [ ... It] is clear that in order for me to be able to devote the time, energy or emotional involvement required in language learning, I must first feel content in the place I am living. My surroundings must be orderly, comfortable and have my imprint on them identifying them as my home away from home. (Schumann & Schumann, 1977: 243–44)

With respect to her experience of language learning in Tunisia, Francine Schumann comments likewise express a deep personal dissatisfaction: 'I hated the method. My anger bred frustration, a frustration which I acutely felt as my goal was to be a star performer in class, and I found it impossible to be so under these circumstances'. She further writes that her reaction

> was to reject [the instructional method] and withdraw from learning. This withdrawal was gradual and displayed itself in a variety of ways. Some days I would assume such a low profile in class, making no attempts to participate, that only my physical presence allowed that I

was indeed a member of the group. Other days this withdrawal took the form of my cutting-up during the lesson. Eventually the withdrawal led to my leaving class early, walking out on exams and on some days not showing up at all. (Schumann & Schumann, 1977: 244)

Schumann contrasts this with her experience in Iran, where 'the accommodations ... lent themselves to [her] fulfilling this [nesting] instinct and doing so within a reasonable period of time' so that 'within a week ... things were to [her] satisfaction [and she] was then able to direct [her] energy to the task of studying Persian' (Schumann & Schumann, 1977: 244). And studying Persian was itself a much more positive experience for her than studying Arabic had been. She studied on her own with her partner, rather than in a classroom setting, and used a combination of American-produced translation readers, which she disliked, and Persian children's books, which (having sought them out on her own and persuaded her partner of their value) she thoroughly enjoyed and found extremely useful linguistically as well as for the cultural insights they provided. She sums up: '[Had] I not been so drawn initially by their beautiful art work we might never have experienced the success or pleasure of learning to read that these children's books ultimately provided' (1977: 245).

What can these comments tell us about Francine Schumann's language-learning process? Can we infer ambivalence or conflict or loss from her experiences? If we cannot draw incontrovertible conclusions from her interpretation of those experiences, we can nevertheless try to poke away a bit at the language of that interpretation. In Tunisia she felt *hostile, frustrated, withdrawn* and *alienated*. Not only was she a foreigner in terms of citizenship, but she was also quite unable to make herself a home, and she could not learn the language. In her words her environment *rejected* her, and she rejected it in return. In short, she could neither find nor make a place for herself, physically or linguistically. By contrast, in Iran she was *comfortable* and *satisfied. Drawn* by the texts she had sought and found, she experienced *pleasure* learning from them. What is the significance of the differences between these two experiences? What can psychoanalysis tell us about them?

To attempt to draw conclusions about the degree to which Schumann's comfort – or lack of comfort – in her environment determined her success or failure in language learning is, of course, a matter of conjecture. We cannot know for certain whether it was her relative contentment in her living situation in Iran that allowed her to seek out texts that she found more beneficial than the ones originally assigned to her. Nor can we do more than speculate about why she did not do something similar in Tunisia, but rather simply withdrew from learning into a kind of stubborn, alienated silence.

Nevertheless, there seems to be a suggestion, implicit in the contrast between the two experiences, that Schumann's sense of belonging, or lack of it, contributed to her ability in one place – and her inability in the other – to learn. In a curious inversion of Winnicott's phenomenon of the split-off intellect, it appears that Schumann's Tunisian experience may have represented a kind of split-off affect, a time of hyper-affect in which, regardless of the goals she had set for acquiring Arabic, her unconscious but dominant affective self prevented her from 'learning [it] in spite of the method' (Schumann & Schumann, 1977: 244) and forced her to 'choose' to withdraw from it. Further, we can, I think, extrapolate from this withdrawal an indication of how the Winnicottian requirement of an 'environmental provision of the holding variety' (Winnicott, 1970: 119) was, for Schumann, lacking in the Tunisian setting but present in Iran. For what can a sense of alienation, of homelessness, be if it is not, in at least some sense, the absence of a holding environment?

Both these general environmental considerations and the structures of Francine Schumann's Tunisian and Iranian language-learning circumstances argue for the same interpretation. In Tunisia she was situated in a language classroom, where 'the TL [target language] was used exclusively as the medium of instruction' (Schumann & Schumann, 1977: 244). This was another reminder of her foreignness, her position as an outsider cut off from her environment, and in a sense alienated from, made alien to, herself. Although such a situation is clearly difficult enough linguistically because of its implications for self expression, I maintain that it may also be reminiscent of more primal moments of being split off from an earlier self, as well as from the means of expression possessed by that self which must be attenuated in the split. Conversely, in Iran Schumann was working with a partner with whom she shared a language. She was using materials of their own choosing, and was in substantially more control of both her own particular learning practices and the degree to which she could integrate, or re-integrate, the learning (intellectual) and being (affective) aspects of herself. If the Lacanian 'fundamental form of alienation that is part and parcel of learning one's mother tongue' (Fink, 1995: 7) can be unconsciously recalled by learning some *other* – someone else's – mother tongue, perhaps the recalling can be ameliorated by holding on to some part of the life that has been lived in that first mother tongue.

Francine Schumann's partner, John Schumann, likewise addresses the question of control over his language-learning experience. He reports his position on this question very succinctly (Schumann & Schumann, 1977:

246): 'I like to have my own agenda in second language learning. In other words, I like to do it my way. However, I also found that my agenda is often in conflict with the teacher's'. He names the fact of conflict in language learning more directly than Francine Schumann does, but the conflict to which he refers is perhaps not as substantively different from hers as it appears at first glance. Both researchers seem to have experienced difficulty in language-learning circumstances in which the wishes of the language-learning *inside* clashed with the apparent aims of the language-teaching *outside*. John Schumann maintains that his 'desire to pursue [his] own agenda was somewhat more successful ... [in a learning environment where he] could choose not to do a writing assignment ... [and his] failure at a [writing] task would not be public' (Schumann & Schumann, 1977: 246). In contrast, his partner recognised the potential value of finding a way of learning 'in spite of the method' (1977: 244), but was nevertheless unable to do so.

John Schumann attributes to his shyness this further observation: 'I prefer eavesdropping to speaking as a way of getting into a language ... [and] I prefer to get input by listening to the TL without having to become involved in a conversation' (Schumann & Schumann, 1977: 247). But what does it really mean to be shy? Without undertaking an exhaustive enquiry into that particular quality of personality, I note that dictionary definitions focus on such descriptors as 'retiring ... easily frightened away ... distrustful [and] wary',[1] 'diffident or uneasy in company', characterised by reserve',[2] all of which are helpful, but which do not elaborate their causes. I wonder about possible connections between Schumann's 'shyness' – insofar as it implies a movement away from (or a refusal to move towards) engagement with others, and his additional assertion that he prefers 'eavesdropping'. He describes this as 'listening to the radio, watching television and participating in events where [he can] hear people speak without having to speak [him]self' (Schumann & Schumann, 1977: 247). This assertion of his preference might be viewed psychoanalytically as an acknowledgement both of his positioning as other to the target language group (and, conversely, of its positioning as other to him) and of the way he responds to his unconscious recognition of a conflict between two competing internal desires. There is the desire, on the one hand to learn the new language and thereby move to a position within its community of speakers, and on the other hand to maintain himself outside that language, as well as, by dint of that outside position, silent with respect to it. Thus surfaces, once again, the conflict between the articulate and the pre- (or previously) articulate selves.

The diary approach to the study of second-language learning originated by Schumann and Schumann was taken up by Kathleen Bailey (1983) in an article that focuses on competitiveness and anxiety as factors in second language learning. Bailey provides interpretations of numerous language-learners' diaries, including one she herself undertook during a French translation course. In contrast with Schumann and Schumann, she also includes excerpts from the diaries alongside her interpretations.

One of Bailey's concerns as a linguist is the generalisability of the diary studies. She notices 'various degrees of introspection and observational acuity among the authors' and makes the judgement that 'some of the studies are more accurate and hence more reliable than others' (Bailey, 1983: 78). In the sense that the diaries are written by different individuals and must necessarily differ from one another in many aspects, she is correct. For my own rather more speculative purposes, however, it is neither necessary nor helpful to make such a judgement. My aim in studying the excerpts is as much to explore what they might merely imply as it is to examine what is manifestly set out in them. There is, therefore, potential usefulness in all of them.

Terence Moore, a British psychologist, kept track of the difficulties he encountered in attempting to learn Danish on the occasion of his appoint-ment as chair of the clinical psychology department at the University of Aarhus. His personal account of that experience (Moore, 1977), and the diary excerpts he includes within it, some of which Bailey (1983) later reviews, speak to his experience of restricted communicative ability as suggestive of aphasia or deafness, and are especially reminiscent of 'the child in the class where the work is too difficult for him' (Moore, 1977: 107). From notes he made following his first class in Danish, Moore quotes: 'This is a good reminder of how a child feels when a lesson goes over his head. One feels bewildered; ashamed and inferior when everyone else appears to understand except oneself ...' (1977: 108).

Notwithstanding his use of the non-specific, third-person pronoun, a psychoanalytic reading of which conveys the sense of a projection – or refusal to recognise and subsequent displacement (Laplanche & Pontalis, 1973: 349) – of his own perception onto some nameless third party, this comment clearly refers to Moore's own experience. It is telling in its acknowledgement of the affective components of his response to an incomprehensible lesson. I suspect that part of what this second language incomprehension recalls is the early incomprehension of the infant who has, as yet, no language. But since adults do not consciously recall that early time, perhaps Moore's analogy is best understood as the closest he can consciously get to noticing what, for Phillips, is an unconscious connection with that moment in his history – and with the ' ... indeterminate place where the bodily self meets that contagion of languages called culture' –

from which speech comes: a connection with the pre-language self that occurs '[e]very time we speak, and perhaps particularly every time we have difficulty speaking – and so get a glimpse of what our fluency conceals ...' (Phillips, 1999: 54–55). The discussion that Moore undertakes subsequent to the learning experience, and also subsequent to the exercise of describing that experience in his journal, seems to support this position. He compares the 'problem of finding the expression that sounds natural and right in the new language' to the aphasic's 'shattered world' and maintains that 'such frustration can be observed wherever command of language is inadequate to frame a message struggling for expression: often in preverbal children, for example' (Moore, 1977: 109). We might well ask just what – or who – it is that is struggling for expression, in the preverbal child or in the second-language learner. Is it only a message, or something – or someone – more?

The concept of the self as other to itself is exemplified by the diary of Hindy Leichman (1977), which narrates the experience of learning Indonesian as a foreign language. Writing in her diary about the uncertain comparisons she is prone to make between her own performance and that of her classmates, Leichman says:

> So many of my hang-ups about language learning were my own percep-tions of what I do and what others do. Unfortunately, I did not know which were distortions of the truth ... So much depended on how I viewed myself and others. Very often I would try to stop concerning myself with how I thought they were doing and try concentrating on me. (Leichman 1977: 3; cited in Bailey, 1983: 84)

While perhaps not quite approaching the 'self-reproaches and self-revilings' that, for Freud (1991: 252), can mark the deterioration of self-regard in the melancholic, there is, in the language of Leichman's diary, and specifically in statements such as 'I *viewed myself*', and 'I would try ... *to concentrate on me*', a hint that she conceives of her second-language-learning self as apart somehow from herself-as-a-whole, perhaps in the more Lacanian sense of the self becoming other to itself, in part through acquiring language. There is also, in Leichman, more than a hint of conflict. She recalls: 'Throughout the course there was a struggle within myself between my old feelings (of failure) and my desire for success' (Leichman, 1977: 6; cited in Bailey, 1983: 84).

Similar to Leichman, another diarist, Marjorie Walsleben (1976), relates her experience of learning Persian in terms of several conflicts. These include conflicts between her desire to learn and her disapproval of the testing method and between having insufficient time to study and her wish to perform well on vocabulary tests. She also relates one particularly long, intensive and 'emotional exchange of opinions dealing with what the class was and was not, what it could and should be, who would let whom do what', in which a conflict arose between her 'belief that [the professor] had heard [the students'] criticisms and suggestions and [her] doubt that he would actually do anything in response to them'. She exclaims, 'I felt exhausted and empty' (Walsleben, 1976: 34–35; cited in Bailey, 1983: 87).

Bailey's assessment of this conflict is that Walsleben 'is struggling with the instructor for control of her language-learning experience' (Bailey, 1983: 87). It is unclear who wins this struggle, if indeed it can be said to be 'won' at all. Walsleben is not only exhausted and empty, but she soon becomes silent and absent, bodily as well as linguistically. Ultimately, she leaves the class outright before the end of the course. This struggle between student and teacher takes on some of the colouring of the conflict between inside and outside that, for Freud, emerges from the individual's first judgement: 'I should like to eat this', or 'I should like to spit it out' (Freud, 1925: 439). Here, the 'this' is not only the way the second language is taught, it is the language itself. And the decision of the learner, in this case, is to refuse to eat and to move away from the second-language table, in spite of her previous determination and desire: 'I had spent hours and hours studying Farsi because I wanted to and was determined to keep progressing ... But suddenly – it did not seem to matter' (Walsleben, 1976: 36; cited in Bailey, 1983: 87).

This conflict between 'taking in' a second language and rejecting it is rooted in the ambivalence of the learner's desire both to learn and to refuse learning that accompanies learning's perpetual state of emergency (Britzman, 1998: 23). It is articulated, within the diary excerpts, in frequent analogies that the diarists make between the relationships of teachers and students and those of parents and children. These analogies also call to mind once again the Freudian concept of the family romance (Freud, 1909), discussed in the previous chapter and entailing, in part, motives of sibling rivalry, among which is a sense in which the child may imagine herself as the product of a clandestine love affair between her mother and a man other than her actual father, or alternatively as the only 'legitimate' child among her siblings.

Rebecca Jones, a student of Indonesian, writes that 'a curious form of sibling rivalry developed among [the students]. Dr. Fox ... functioned in the role of the parent with all of the learners acting as children, competing to achieve recognition and attention ...' (1977: 77). For Deborah Plummer, initially, a similar analogy provides a way to think positively about her experience:

The best way I can describe my psychological state in the class is child-like ... I was expected to bring to the class no previous knowledge of the language ... [The teacher] became very much of a parental figure to me, in whom I could place my trust ... [During] class I was an adult who struggled to talk about elementary concrete objects in the most simple, childlike speech. Instead of being frustrated by such a dichotomy, I found it much easier to adopt a childlike identity in the new language ... [This] new identity helped preserve my adult ego and self-confidence. (Plummer, 1976: 5–6; cited in Bailey, 1983: 90)

But Plummer's childlike state is interrupted. Eventually she notices

an abrupt change from the in-class parental figure. In and out of class [the teacher] was a person I highly respected and from whom I sought recognition and approval – as if she were a parent ... I felt that I had lost her recognition, approval and favour. I lost my self-confidence and most of all I lost my childlike feeling. I was an adult ... responsible for my actions and my L2 errors became ego deflating and wounding. (Plummer, 1976: 8–9; cited in Bailey, 1983: 91)

Plummer's eventual reporting of the satisfactory resolution of her problem further substantiates this idea of her sense of – and her pleasure and unpleasure in – her teacher as a parental figure. What ultimately satisfies her need for approval is a renewal in 'self-worth and acceptance from [her] parental figure. She [the teacher] was more sensitive to [Plummer's] needs in class and her subtle attention, unnoticed by others, was very encouraging' (Plummer, 1976: 8–9; cited in Bailey, 1983: 91).

Not all the diary excerpts make explicit connections between second language learning–teaching relationships and the relationships between children and their parents. Still, in addition to the passages quoted above, numerous statements concerning the students' desires to perform well for, be flattered by, and generally please their teachers (Walsleben, 1976; Jones, 1977; Leichman, 1977) carry echoes of the child's wish to please her parents – itself arguably a wish that harks back to the pre-language, undifferentiated infant. Moreover, the role of the teacher in imposing authority, as a kind of superego-once-removed, is a comparison readily drawn from the articulation of such desires. And, of course, desires are subject to resistance on the part of the unconscious (in this case that of the learner). Indeed, it seems reasonable to suspect that the criticisms of teaching methods articulated by some of the diary excerpts (Walsleben, 1976; Jones, 1977; Schumann, 1977) might represent sublimated resistances to precisely that parental/pedagogical control.

Psychoanalytically interpreted, the portions of the Jones (1977) and Plummer (1976) diaries examined above – and to a lesser extent those of

Leichman (1977) and Walsleben (1976) – share characteristics with a narrative that Ehrman and Dörnyei (1998) include in their discussion. They suggest that this narrative might exemplify a psychoanalytic *transference*, a 'particular instance of displacement of affect from one idea to another' (Laplanche & Pontalis, 1973: 457) – a situation in which 'infantile prototypes re-emerge and are experienced with a strong suggestion of immediacy' (1973: 455). Ehrman and Dörnyei quote a student's articulation of his disappointment in a particular teacher, and then offer a psychoanalytic 'translation' of the student's comments. I set out here, first, a brief excerpt from the student's comments:

> I was irritated by the fact that he looked on certain people as if they automatically knew everything ... [N]othing at first really showed that they knew more than I did, or the others in the class ... I guess that teacher started it all, and then all the others started talking about the differences, which were no big differences at all. I felt the opinion of the teacher about those two people was an impenetrable category... (Ehrman & Dörnyei, 1998: 59–60)

And the same excerpt, psychoanalytically interpreted by the authors (with changed words in round brackets):

> I was irritated by the fact that (my father) looked on (my brother and sister) as if they automatically knew everything ... nothing really [...]showed that they (were better than I was), or the others in (my family). [...]I guess (my father) started it all, and then all the others started talking about the differences, which were no big differences at all. I felt the opinion of (my father) about those two people was an impenetrable category ... (Ehrman & Dörnyei, 1998: 61)

Acknowledging the speculative nature of their claims, the authors nevertheless argue that this particular student may be

> *unconsciously* projecting a situation of sibling rivalry onto his class based on his previous experiences in his family of origin ... and is experiencing the teacher/father as liking his classmates/siblings best. (Ehrman & Dörnyei, 1998: 61–62; italics in original)

My own readings of the diary excerpts are similarly speculative. However, with Ehrman and Dörnyei, I maintain that while a psychoanalytically-focused reading of an individual's comments is selective rather than exhaustive it may nevertheless be helpful, especially in situations, as set out in some of the diaries, in which 'an individual's response seems inappropriate to what stimulated it' (Ehrman & Dörnyei, 1998: 62).

There is one more aspect of the diaries that I wish to explore. First, however, it is important to offer a brief word concerning my rationale for doing so. As explained earlier, my discussion in most cases makes reference to and analyses excerpts previously selected by Bailey from the original diaries, rather than the diary texts as a whole. Bailey, in turn, chose these excerpts for their relevance to her work on anxiety and competitiveness. Moreover, language is clearly a social activity, and the language-learner diaries are, in most cases, undertaken by students within a group learning context. It is thus not surprising that the excerpts include substantial references to the diarists' classmates, and to the diarists' perceptions of the learning experiences of their classmates. By the same token, however, while I cannot know with absolute certainty the original intention of the journals themselves (that is, the intentions of the journal-writers), it does seem somewhat unexpected that these diaries, which by generally-understood definition would be expected to recount one's *own* experiences and affective responses, so readily provide the kind of data that Bailey took from them.

To be precise, I am struck by the apparently frequent inclusion of what psychoanalysis might argue as a projection – for Freud the means by which the 'system *Cs.* [consciousness] protects itself' against 'instinctual danger' (Freud, 1915b: 187). Here in the diaries, what is defended against is conflict, anxiety and struggle, and this is, in my view, projected by the diarists on to their fellow learners. In addition to the experience of Terence Moore (1977, as recounted in Bailey, 1983), this observation perhaps more surprisingly includes Bailey's own diary, which she explores in her 1983 paper. Here Bailey sets out the aim of the language-learner diaries: to attempt to speak to the problem, 'How can a classroom researcher discover what individual students really do and think and feel during the language lesson?' (Bailey, 1983: 71). She does not explicitly invite the diarists to interpret what *other* learners might be doing and thinking and feeling. And, as it happens, although Bailey does not state outright that in undertaking her diary she had any specific research objectives in mind, she does express surprise at the realisation of her own competitiveness, which she notices as a result of her frequent comparisons in her diary between herself and the other students in the class (1983: 73). In short, there is something of a gap between the 'database for studying personal and affective variables in language learning' that Bailey wanted to *make with* her diary, and the surprising revelations of competitiveness and concern with classmates that she *found in* it. The diaries offer data. The gap offers justification for my approach to those data, which is to address the projected conflict and ambivalence that I find in (and/or, arguably, make of), Bailey's diary as such and her retrospective interpretation of it.

'It appears', writes Bailey in the analysis of her diary excerpts, 'that during the first two weeks of the ten-week course I was highly anxious about learning French because I felt I could not compete with the other students' (Bailey, 1983: 74). Another reading of the excerpts is equally compelling, however. Having studied, three years earlier, introductory French for two terms, Bailey was not at the very beginning of the second language acquisition process. Nevertheless, although her diary excerpts give no explicit evidence of a textbook manifestation of a silent period, or a silence as such, they do suggest that the anxiety expressed in them may have been rooted somewhere other than in mere concern about competing with other students – somewhere deeper, unnoticed consciously, and consequently silent in the writing of the diary. Several trends within the excerpts lead me to this view. One of these is Bailey's striking tendency to attribute discomfort and frustration to her classmates, as illustrated by the following comments, written after the first and second classes (and portions of which I have emphasised):

> ... [The teacher] often writes on the board when she sees we don't understand what she has said ... I am interested in the problems of *one man in the class who ... is desperate and somewhat discouraged.* I hope I can encourage him. He is really trying. He talked to the teacher after class but *he's using a lot of energy fighting with his own frustrations* ... (Bailey, 1983: 74)

> ... Today I was panicked in the oral exercise where we had to fill in the blanks ... *Now I know what ESL students go through* ... (Bailey, 1983: 74)

> ... I'm probably the second lowest in the class right now (next to the man who must pass the ETS test). The girl who has been in France seems to think that she's too good for the rest of us, but she didn't do all that well today ... Today I was just scared enough to be stimulated to prepare for next time. If I were any scareder I'd be a nervous wreck. I feel different from many of the students in the class because they have been together for a quarter with the other teacher. They also don't seem very interested in learning French. Today ... some of the students looked really bored. (Bailey, 1983: 75)

A few observations: in the first of these early diary entries Bailey assumes incomprehension on the part of other students – '*we* don't understand what *she* [the teacher] has said'. In the second entry, a brief acknowledgement of Bailey's own anxiety – she calls it panic – is quickly followed and thereby de-emphasised by comments about the difficulties she attributes to others in her class. And in the third, she claims a position at the 'low' end of the spectrum of student achievement within the class, and briefly mentions her fear, but these comments are at once glossed over, thereby effectively denying themselves. By articulating how frightened she is *not*, that is, by making the claim that she is *not quite* a nervous wreck, she minimises the significance of her previous statement that in fact she is afraid. Each of the excerpts reserves its most lengthy and detailed discussion for the discomforts perceived (I contend through projection) as experienced by others. And all this talk about others is a kind of non-talk, a silence, about herself. Simply put, my argument is that Bailey cannot fully express her own difficulties in her diary, except by attributing them to other learners; with regard to her own difficulties she is, in effect, almost speechless.

This speechlessness changes somewhat, however, in Bailey's subsequent discussion of these same excerpts. In this later moment, of Bailey reading Bailey, and Bailey interpreting Bailey, she locates her earlier self as a 'learner who was very uncomfortable and extremely anxious' (Bailey, 1983: 75). In retrospect, she attributes the feelings articulated in her diary, and those not quite articulated but rather attributed to others, to the competitive aspects of her personality. And while it is not my aim to use psychoanalytic theory either to flatten all of the complexities or to claim full understanding of Bailey's or anyone else's language-learning experience, I am compelled to suggest that perhaps this 'competitiveness' explanation, offered by Bailey-the-linguist on behalf of Bailey-the-diarist, is itself still not quite complete.

My justification for making this claim rests, like my reasons for initially proposing Bailey's metaphorical silence, in the diary excerpts. By the fourth session, Bailey had already skipped a class. Worth quoting at length, here is how her diary relates that episode:

> Last Friday after class I spoke to [the teacher] and apologised for slowing down the class. I asked her how far they had gone the previous quarter ... so that I could try to catch up over the weekend ... I had planned to do a total review of the French grammar book, but I didn't get to it because I had so much departmental business to do. [On Sunday night] I began reading the assigned chapter but I got bogged down and discouraged and I quit. Coming to school today I vowed to leave my office an hour before class so I could prepare. Some things came up though and twenty minutes before the class was supposed to start, I decided to skip class and use the time to review instead. Then I discovered that I had left my French books at home! I know I am (or can be) a good language learner, but I hate being lost in class ... Since I didn't have the French books, I decided to go to the library and study for my other class ... I tried to read

but I was so upset about the French class that I couldn't concentrate so I've just been writing in my journal. I *must* get caught up in French or I'll never be able to go back to the class. (Bailey, 1979: 43–44; italics in original)

This fascinating passage reads like an inventory of troubles. Bailey asserts that she knows (although she immediately qualifies that knowledge) that she is a good language learner who has, owing to circumstances, fallen behind. She *must* catch up, but somehow, on this particular occasion, things keep happening that prevent her from doing so. She loses time working on unrelated matters; when she does tackle her French she soon becomes discouraged; she again sets aside time, and then realises, when it is too late to do anything about it, that she has forgotten the materials she needs.

Later excerpts recount how, in a test situation within the same course, Bailey was pleased with the fact that she finished early. However, when the exam was returned she was surprised to realise that she had, apparently inadvertently, missed completing a substantial part of it. Interestingly, her diary entry on the day the test was written refers to that very section. In her later analysis of her diary she mentions this curious fact, observing: 'I *had* noticed those parts of the test; otherwise I wouldn't have been able to describe them in the entry ... The diary shows that I had ... been aware ... at some point during the test' of the questions missed (Bailey, 1983: 76).

Certainly it is possible to interpret this lapse, and those outlined in the preceding passage, as accidents, as what in common parlance might be called 'innocent mistakes'. But for psychoanalysis 'there is nothing innocent about forgetting, slips of the tongue, jokes, indeed all forms of parapraxis – those bungled actions that point elsewhere even as they can be observed as interfering with daily life' (Britzman, 1998: 68). Anna Freud explains:

Examining the small mistakes in the everyday life of human beings, such as forgetting, losing, or misplacing things, misreading or mishearing, psychoanalysis succeeded in demonstrating that such errors are always based on an intent of the person who makes them ... Psychoanalytic investigation established that, generally speaking, we forget nothing except what we wish to forget for some good reason or other, though that reason is usually quite unknown to us. (A. Freud, 1974: 81–82)

And Ehrman and Dörnyei expand on this noting that, according to the psychoanalytic principle of *psychic determinism*, 'behaviour is meaningful and not random or accidental ...' and 'individuals ... [unconsciously] give each other messages about their feelings and wishes' (Ehrman & Dörnyei,

1998: 11). Both Bailey's failure to notice part of her test, and the account of her attempt, thwarted many times, to catch up on her studying, can be read as a series of unconscious acts of avoidance that point at a psychical conflict within her, between a wish to learn French and a wish to avoid it, and that subsequently communicate this conflicted feeling to the reader of her diary. The story of her attempt at studying shares a helpless, powerless quality with the kind of dream it so directly resembles – in which the dreamer is prevented by external forces from accomplishing a goal she consciously believes she desires. If, as psychoanalysis contends, a dream is the fulfilment of a wish, perhaps this narrative, so dreamlike in its qualities, may likewise contain within it the kernel of a wish. For the obstacles to Bailey's studying can be understood psychoanalytically as originating within her, and by extension, however entertaining they might be to read about, as manifestations of that conflict, by now familiar, between 'the desire to learn and the desire to ignore', the desire that fights against learning (Britzman, 1998: 5).

Hand in hand with this conflict, and the ambivalence arising from it, goes a second struggle. Like the previous one it is present in the acquisition of a first language, and like the first one it persists in the learning of a second language. It is that conflict between the self's longing for communication and unity (however attenuated the possibility for communication and unity might be) and its equally compelling longing to maintain the integrity of what Pitt, following Winnicott, has called the 'permanently isolated and secret self' (Pitt, 2000: 65). Neither alternative is what we want, or all that we want: we want, and do not want, both at once, and to opt for one is to refuse the other.

An additional connection between the ambivalent wish on the part of the self to reveal itself and, at the same time, to keep its secret (Pitt, 2000) is conveyed in Colette Soler's discussion of Lacan's symbolic order. Soler states (1996: 41–42) that speech, for Lacan, functions dually, as both mediation and revelation. Speech-as-mediation works within the realm of the ego: its aim is 'to establish a link with the other, that is, the alter ego ... someone who can understand you ... and who can know something about you'. What is more, she emphasises that 'the function of mediation *unites* one with the other. That is, in this uniting, we can extract a link, but not a mere link: a link that is essentially unifying...' (Soler, 1996: 42; italics in original). Still, there is a struggle, and there is ambivalence. The aim of language-as-mediation may be unity, but it is an aim laden with conflict and compromised from the start. We cannot return to the unity of self and other that existed before the primal separation and before language, and on some level we know this: there is no going home – not to that home, anyway. The self that pursues language as a way to win back that early inarticulate unity is chasing its own tail. All it can really do is to try to create, and make do with, a severely attenuated semblance of that unity; and this it must achieve with, through – even in spite of – language.

Learning a second language has a similar aim, but its conflict and compromise are doubled. Like the self who is learning a first language, the second-language-learning self seeks a unity it can achieve only in attenuated form. But here the attenuation is exacerbated. For standing between the second-language self in search of unity and the inarticulate state of unity that it unconsciously and nostalgically seeks is the first-language self, that interminable reminder that outright unity is impossible, and that the more one uses language to try to attain unity the more fragmented one might likely end up. Neither fish nor fowl, neither unified nor potentially fully unifying, the first-language self gestures at the impossibility of the very wish it sought to fulfil, but could not – the same wish that the second-language-learning self now seeks to fulfil, and cannot.

So what is to be done? If we listen to what psychoanalytic theory has to say, it seems that, as a methodology for communication, language satisfies our wishes only partly at best, because it cannot serve the persistent desires of our non-speaking, pre-language selves except inadvertently and in a diluted fashion. And yet, it may be all we have. To make matters even more troubling, at the same time it seems that we are not quite certain about what our desires actually are. This chapter has tried to listen to the stories of human selves as they learn new languages in an effort to find new ways of making relations with the world, and of making the links with others that Soler (1996: 42) has called 'essentially unifying'. It has also tried to take up some of the hints offered by psychoanalytic theory in order to listen to the sub-texts of those stories – the desires and the conflicts and the ambivalence in second language learning. For the struggle, between the longing to be known and to communicate and the opposing desire to 'defend against communication with the secret self' (Pitt 2000: 65), persists through the language learning process and into the recounting of that process. It is a struggle not easily related. But by helping us to listen to the silences behind the words, and to take the hints that live in the spaces between the lines, psychoanalytic theory may have helped us hear a little of it: for even in the silence of the untold story, the unconscious speaks.

## Notes

1. *Random House Webster's College Dictionary,* 2nd edn, *s.v.* 'shy'.
2. *The Canadian Oxford Dictionary, s.v.* 'shy'.

## Chapter 5
# Taking the Hint: Working with Silence

*Shall we admit that something other than consciousness*
*interferes with education?*
Deborah Britzman
*Lost Subjects, Contested Objects:*
*Toward a Psychoanalytic Inquiry of Learning, 1998*

*The living individual is a system of individuation, an individuating*
*system and also a system that individuates itself. The internal resonance*
*and the translation of its relation to itself into information are all*
*contained in the living being's system.*
Gilbert Simondon
*The Genesis of the Individual, 1992*

Adam Phillips' metaphor describing the language of children as a route 'back to bodies' (Phillips, 1999: 29), that is to an organismic wholeness paradoxically both lost and regained in the movement into speech, is given a new resonance when read alongside Roland Barthes's meditation on language as somehow corporeal: 'Language is a skin: I rub my language against the other. It is as if I had words instead of fingers, or fingers at the tip of my words' (Barthes, 1978: 73). The evocative language in Barthes's version of the metaphor brings us, once more, back through words to bodies.

But not just to our own bodies – for, if we play a little with Barthes's words, we can wonder how the skin-that-is-language rubs against the skin of another, the other's language. Our skin touches the skin of the other, yet it also holds us within ourselves, holds our selves within us, within the *'individuating system that individuates itself'* that for Gilbert Simondon constitutes the *'living individual'* (Simondon, 1992: 305; italicised in orig-inal). It is what keeps us contained, but it also touches the world, at once both connecting us and preventing our connection with what is other to us – both on the inside and on the outside.

So too does our language touch the language of the other. Yet it also holds us within ourselves, holds our selves within us. We might think about a second language as a kind of second skin, enveloping the first, separating us by a second layer from what is other to us, but incorporating at the same time a second set of nerve endings, twice as much feeling, intensifying the longing for connection with that other.

This book has taken a multidisciplinary approach to the notion of the individual in the process of acquiring a second language, as partly constituted and partly contained by a language-as-a-skin, through reading narratives that speak (though not always deliberately) to the question of silence in second language learning. Following several theoretical paths, each for a time, and endeavouring to attend to the guideposts along the way, this work has reflected on some of the hints those theories offer, accumulating useful concepts, trying new ways of reading, and asking new questions.

The road has taken some interesting and unexpected turns. For, in order to engage with silence in second language learning, it was imperative first to try to grab hold of the elusive fact of silence, and then to engage its qualities in several of their various guises. Next came the task of speculating about some of the meanings of those various silences, a speculation that I have maintained can come about, to a meaningful extent, through taking up hints offered by the learner. To that end I have turned an interpretive lens on to examples of two kinds of autobiographical writing: memoirs and diaries. Written by diverse and differently-motivated individuals from varied linguistic, social and cultural backgrounds, these narratives have provided a rich and in many ways remarkably consistent source of such hints, which I have nudged into dialogue with other cues, proffered by other discourses: in this study, primarily psychoanalytic theory, helped along by SLA research and social constructivist theories of identity. Now I speak a little more directly to some issues of pedagogical praxis that concern the second language learning process – and silence in that process – within the context of education. In so doing I give specific consideration to how educators and learners might use these conjectures to make meaning for themselves.

In her work on the interference that is education, Britzman (1998: 5) asks how education lives in people and, conversely, how people live within education. To recast that question within the overarching framework of this study is to give it a somewhat Lacanian flavour: how does *language* live in people, and how do people live in *language*? It is also to gesture towards a new and differently articulated version of this question, as an exploration of what silence might tell us about how, in learning a second language, people and language live inside and outside each other. And so I ask my own question, a pointedly pedagogical one that is about language learning and also about education writ large: How can education think about and engage with the many ways in which second-language learners live the various silences of their learning?

At first blush, to begin to answer that question recalls the old joke that asks, 'How do you pet a porcupine?' – and its answer, 'Very, very carefully'. But the field of SLA research has put forward some pedagogical approaches that, while they do not articulate precisely the same speculations I have made in this book concerning silence, might nevertheless be thought of as offering a response to them. In turn, some of these responses have been taken up by educational practice.

Gibbons' (1985: 265) suggestion that early second language curriculum 'should consist of a reduced output stage' in terms of the demands made on learners *vis-à-vis* target language production, reflects the view articulated by Dulay *et al.* (1982), that 'one-way or restricted two-way communication ... is a kind of self-imposed constraint which language learners, both first and second, seem to require in order for the acquisition process to unfold most naturally' (1982: 23). Dulay *et al.* (1982: 23–26) also outline several teaching methods that provide for, or even insist on, an initial period of silence. Among these, the 'Total Physical Response' (TPR) method requires that 'during approximately the first ten hours ... students remain silent but are required to obey teacher commands [made] in the target language' (1982: 23–24). Another method, named the 'Natural Approach', maintains that:

> a student is likely to try to speak in the new language whenever he or she makes a decision to do so, i.e. whenever his or her self-image and ease in the classroom is such that a response in the second language will not produce anxiety. (Terrell, 1977: 333)

The Natural Approach method allows students to choose to use their first language until they reach a level of comfort such that they decide, on their own, to use the target language.

Such methods, especially the Natural Approach, seem to foreshadow the more recent movement, within SLA research and theory, towards a curriculum based on understanding rather than on production. The comprehension-based approach to second language learning and instruction emphasises the development of comprehension through listening, and does not insist on learner production until 'students understand and internalise more and more of the target language, thereby forming a fund on which they can draw to speak and write' (Robert Courchêne, 1992: 97).

More recently still, the position of the National Association for the Education of Young Children (NAEYC) in the United States includes the following reference to a silent period in the second language acquisition process:

Just as children learn and develop at different rates, individual differences exist in how children whose home language is not English acquire English. For example, some children may experience a silent period (of six or more months) while they acquire English ... Each child's way of learning a new language should be viewed as acceptable, logical, and part of the ongoing development and learning of any new language. (NAEYC, 1995)

The general pedagogical views embodied in the comprehension-based approach are a beginning. Though focused explicitly on language comprehension and not on psychical readiness, they nevertheless allow the learner some latitude in determining when to commence production. Conceivably, they might be extended to incorporate the recognition of psychical factors (such as the kinds of conflict and ambivalence engaged in this study) that may, in some learners, contribute to or detract from the acquisition of comprehension and the development of a readiness to begin target language production, as well as the ways these factors assert themselves differently for individual learners.

Together these pedagogical models – reduced output, Total Physical Response, the Natural Approach, and comprehension-based methods in general – point to the rubric of *learner autonomy*. This is a concept that harmonises with the current focus on learner-centredness in education, itself anticipated by the work of, among others, John Dewey (1956), Maria Montessori (1964) and Carl Rogers, who in 1961 put forward the view that 'self-discovered, self-appropriated learning' is the most valuable (Rogers, 1995: 276). More recently, the concept of learner autonomy, initially a response to the question of how adult education might cultivate individuals' freedom and responsibility as both creators and products of society (Henri Holec, 1981: 1), has been brought into relation with – and indeed into practice within – multiple levels and aspects of education. Generally, it emphasises the ability of learners 'to set learning goals and to organise their own learning activity' (David Crabbe, 1999: 3). David Little offers a more detailed definition:

[The] *basis* of learner autonomy is acceptance of responsibility for one's own learning; the *development* of learner autonomy depends on the exercise of that responsibility in a never-ending effort to understand what one is learning, why one is learning, how one is learning, and with what degree of success; and the *effect* of learner autonomy is to remove the barriers that so easily erect themselves between formal learning and the wider environment in which the learner lives. (Little, 1999: 11; italics in original)

Those who promote learner autonomy as a theory that can inform practice are quick to recognise the complexities not only in its implications for practice but also in its very origins. Holec carefully notes, for example, that, while the autonomous learner does direct his or her own learning, it is not necessarily the case that all self-directed learners are autonomous: 'different degrees of self-direction in learning may result either from different degrees of autonomy or from different degrees of exercise of autonomy' (Holec, 1981: 4). And, following Holec, Phil Benson and Peter Voller (Benson & Voller, 1997) point out that, while commonly considered in relation to the internal processes and outward behaviours of individuals, the concepts of autonomy and self-determination as applied to language learning are rooted in the ideas of, among others, Paulo Freire (1970) and Ivan Illich (1971). According to Benson and Voller (1997: 5), in these philosophies, which regard learning as potentially liberatory, autonomy 'has a more radical, social content concerned not only with the psychological autonomy of the individual, but also with the autonomy of individuals as they are constituted within social groups'. Implementing it in relation to second language learning, by extension, involves 'ambiguities arising from ... tensions ... between responsibility and freedom from constraint ... and between the individual and the social' (1997: 5)

Benson and Voller's acknowledgement of the multiple factors and influences bearing on the work of developing learner autonomy recalls Harré's (1993) socially-informed theorising of autonomy and Winnicott's (1967) psychoanalytic understanding of the autonomous individual as one who has experienced adequate environmental holding. Both Harré and Winnicott emphasise, in their different yet complementary ways, the multiple interrelationships between individuals and the world in which they live, move, make meaning, and are themselves made and remade, over and over again. Coupled with Little's (1999) explanation that learner autonomy works towards overcoming barriers between formal language learning encounters and the environment as a whole, their work invites us to consider other barriers, between the individual and the external learning environment (whatever its configuration). It also points to Ehrman and Dörnyei's reminder that, in psychotherapy and in education, the 'relationship between leader (therapist or teacher) and patient or student is affected by both *conscious* and *unconscious processes*' (Ehrman & Dörnyei, 1998: 16; emphasis in original).

But Little himself (1999) seems to focus primarily on events and processes of which the learner is – or at least becomes – conscious. Following his definition of learner autonomy, quoted above, he goes on to specify that 'autonomy is a capacity for a certain range of highly explicit (that is, conscious) behaviour that embraces both the process and the content of learning' (Little, 1999: 11). Elsewhere, supported by George Kelly's (1963) personal-construct psychology, Little stresses the importance of a process of uncovering or developing, in the teacher and the learner as in the psychotherapy client, 'a capacity for conscious autonomy' (Little, 1991: 20). This emphasis on conscious awareness and behaviour seems as significant for what it merely implies as for what it states outright, namely the idea that, in both teacher and learner, there may be something other than consciousness, something quite inaccessible *to* consciousness, that influences both their relations with each other and their individual, internal processes, and that acts as another kind of barrier – one separating internal aspects of individuals themselves.

That noted, the concept of learner autonomy does seem to open up the possibility for new ways of thinking about the relationships between, and the roles of, learner and teacher. It does this by seeking to create, in the language classroom or other learning environment, 'the conditions in which learning proceeds by negotiation, interaction, and problem-solving, rather than by telling and showing' (Little, 1991: 48). Such a process recognises that, while the teacher's responsibility for, say, the selection of course texts, which is based on knowledge and expertise, must not be relinquished outright, it is also the case that 'only learners can know what materials – from whatever source – are genuinely relevant to them' (1991: 49). Thus, in this aspect, as in others, the promotion of learner autonomy means that the traditional role of the teacher (or adviser) must be altered such that the power structure in the classroom is also changed (1991: 44). Such changes to the dynamics of relations between teachers and learners are reflected in the use within the literature on learner autonomy of the terms *adviser, facilitator* or *counsellor* rather than, or in addition to, *teacher* (Little, 1991; Riley, 1997, 1999; Voller, 1997).

But if in some educational circumstances the learner autonomy approach may be part of a solution, it also embodies aspects that in certain settings, particularly those in which some learners are silent, may be problematic. For while it is theoretically possible to acknowledge the intrapersonal factors or aspects of identity (including unconscious influences on learning) that affect a learner's readiness to speak, and to do so from an attitude of non-judgemental acceptance, or what Carl Rogers' student Stanley Standal (1954) named 'unconditional positive regard' (Rogers, 1995: 283), making such an acknowledgement would mean honouring not only silence but also the right of the individual to determine how and when – and indeed whether – that silence should end. Ehrman and Dörnyei, in reminding us that the balance of power in teacher–learner relations falls more heavily on the side of the teacher, who bears 'the initial responsibility for establishing an atmosphere of unconditional positive regard' (Ehrman & Dörnyei, 1998: 46), call for the promotion of learner autonomy and self-regulated learning through the use of a 'democratic teaching style' (1998: 258). And indeed, the view of learner autonomy advanced by Benson and Voller (1997: 2) explicitly articulates the importance of the right of learners 'to determine the direction of their own learning' (see also Little & Dam, 1998; Isson, Kjisik, & Nordlund, 1997). By extension, if educators, and education writ large, are to take seriously the idea that learners should determine the pace and the content of their own learning, it must also tolerate the possibility of moments, of whatever duration, in which that determination is, or seems to be, away from learning (Britzman, 1998).

But day-to-day pedagogical practices, as well as the myriad social and institutional demands made manifest in curricula that direct those practices, are not always quite so generous. Thus the same features and aims that make learner autonomy and other learner-centred pedagogical paradigms worthwhile also make them difficult to achieve. For under-standings of what education is supposed to be and to do, which are deeply enmeshed with the roles and characteristics that teachers and learners ascribe to one another – in a process of categorisation that Riley (1999: 38) calls 'membershipping' – are grounded in the individual, in the institution of education, and in society at large. And as interconnected as they are, it is, admittedly, rather difficult to tease apart these components of the educational mix. Still, it is useful to examine them briefly, in an attempt to convey the sense of how difficult it is for education and educators to engage (or even to tolerate) silence within the second language acquisition process.

At the classroom level, both teachers and learners come to any pedagog-ical encounter with their own complicated sets of personal constructs (Little, 1991: 21–22). These constructs are constituted from individual, social and pedagogical histories, and comprise deeply (if often uncon-sciously) held ideas concerning what teaching and learning – which in the language classroom include speaking and silence – ought to mean (Little, 1991; Voller, 1997; Riley, 1999). Scollon and Scollon's (1981) study provides a concise illustration of the tensions that can arise between the expectations that teachers and students have of each other. They observe that, in a situation in which the teacher is an English speaker and the learner is Atha-baskan,

> the teacher expects to be in charge, to be in the dominant role, but at the
> same time expects the child to display his abilities. The child, on the

other hand, either expects the teacher to be the exhibitionist while he is the spectator, or if the child becomes the exhibitionist, he expects to be treated as the dominant member of the pair. (Scollon & Scollon, 1981: 17)

It is not hard to understand how contradictory expectations such as these, grounded in socially driven and culturally distinct relations of dominance and subordination, might inform a teacher's response to silence, however caused, on the part of a student. Further, it is difficult *not* to see how the belief on the part of a teacher that (as some English speakers apparently believe of Athabaskans) an individual who is silent must be 'unsure, aimless, incompetent, and withdrawn' (Scollon & Scollon, 1981: 21) might well have an impact on the relations between teacher and learner.

Amy Tsui (1996) has also written about teachers' intolerance of silence in second language classrooms. Beginning with the observation that 'getting students to respond in the classroom is a problem that most ESL teachers face' (Tsui, 1996: 145), she further comments that many educators 'dislike or are afraid of silence and ... feel very uneasy or impatient when they fail to get a response from students' (1996: 151). This dislike or fear is quite understandable, for silence can disrupt not only a lesson but also the deeply held personal constructs of the participants in that lesson about the particular learning that ought to be taking place. Implicit in those understandings are assumptions about who has power, and what that power consists of, in the teacher–learner relationship (Ehrman & Dörnyei, 1998: 46).

The kinds of response to silence that Tsui (1996) writes about can also be read psychoanalytically, as a kind of psychical disappointment that comes about when the other (in this case the learner) fails to meet expectations, when she or he does not meet the teacher's need or desire to be responded to, *as* a teacher, in a particular way. Put differently, if one 'is' a teacher, that is if one categorises (Riley, 1999) oneself as *teacher*, what does a learner who apparently cannot or will not learn imply about that identity?

It is clear from this that there exists a significant degree of overlap among the intrapersonal and the interpersonal, the societal and the institutional. For, in addition to being personal and interrelational (a concern of teacher, and learner, and teacher-and-learner together), the issue of silence in second language learning is also a logistical one, framed in the ongoing institutional demands of education. That is, in addition to teachers' affective responses (to their students, whether silent or otherwise; to their interactions with those students; and to the difficulty of understanding and working with silence), institutional demands for language production are at play. These include the curricular and assessment mandates that are informed by, but also contribute to, the social and pedagogical construction of silence as problematic. And so, if the objective of language education, and therefore by implication the aim of the language teacher, is language production, we should not be surprised that classroom practice tends to reflect this normalised construction.

Curricula make concrete the normalised construction of silence as troublesome, and specifically as an obstacle to successful learning. Most often originating with governments, school boards and other authorities removed to varying degrees from the ongoing relations between teachers and learners, curricular requirements and programming mandates (which can include methodological demands, compulsory content, and required outcomes) may together constitute what Brown (1994b: 129) calls 'the biggest hurdle' that teachers (and by implication learners) must overcome.

Further, in a curious – and ironically silent – twist, curricula may simply neglect to acknowledge the potential complexity of learners' responses to the demands made of them. For example, the Ontario Curriculum for French as a Second Language (FSL) for Grade 9 (the last grade in which it is compulsory) and Grade 10 (when it becomes optional) allows that 'students ... should have an adequate 'listening period' before they are expected to communicate in French' (Ontario Ministry of Education and Training, 1999a). The fact that a pre-production 'listening period' is even mentioned in the FSL document is peculiar, given that instruction in French as a Second Language begins, in almost all cases, at least several years before Grade 9, and in some cases begins as early as kindergarten. It would seem that this curriculum document must tolerate a very significant silent (or 'listening') period indeed. But what is more surprising still is that, in contrast, the corresponding document dealing with English as a Second Language and English Literacy Development (ESL/ELD) (Ontario Ministry of Education and Training, 1999b) which, in light of Ontario's significant multicultural population and the dominance of the English language in the province, would seem to apply to a very significant number of students, makes no such specific recognition. Its acknowledgement of learners' individual needs, and of the fact that it takes time to learn a language, is limited to the following directive:

> Programs must be flexible in order to accommodate the needs of students who require instruction in English as a second language or English literacy development, and teachers of all subjects are responsible for helping students develop their ability to use English. Appropriate modifications to teaching, learning, and evaluation strategies must be made to help students gain proficiency in English, since students taking English as a second language at the secondary level have limited time in which to develop this proficiency. Teachers should keep in mind that it

may take up to seven years for a student to acquire a level of proficiency in reading, writing, and abstract thinking in a second language that is on a par with the level mastered by speakers of a first language. (Ontario Ministry of Education and Training, 1999b)

Clearly, it is useful for educators to be reminded that second language acquisition is a complex and lengthy process, and some teachers might indeed read a directive such as the one above as permission to treat – and teach – individual students based on their perceived individual needs rather than only on curricular objectives. Left out of this reminder, however, is an explicit acknowledgement of the tensions that arise when modifications to programs for student learning result in a failure, on the part of students or teachers, to meet curricular requirements, or in a shortage of documented or documentable evidence that those requirements have been met. For part of the reason for the construction of silence as problematic for second language pedagogy are the demands made by education (as a complex social institution that in turn answers to the demands of the community and society it serves) to measure, assess and evaluate – and its concomitant need for a pedagogical product that can be measured, assessed and evaluated. The tensions resulting from a failure to meet those needs might mean that, at times, the work of negotiating teacher–student relations, with a view to supporting the needs of individual learners (whether in a formally circumscribed framework such as learner autonomy, or otherwise), is simply overwhelming, even without taking into account the additional, potentially staggering problems inherent in negotiation itself when language is not present.

Thus the second-language learner's silence can be a problem for educators too, caught between their own pedagogical visions, the individual needs of their students, and the externally-imposed demands of curricula. By and large curriculum policies and documents, and consequently classroom practice, seem to operate implicitly within the same 'common-sense' metaphors of silence that were noted at the beginning of this study as informing some SLA research: an empty container in want of filling, an awkward or even harmful moment that needs to be ended, a wilful, stubborn recalcitrance that must be broken. Consequently, although it is ironic, it is not altogether surprising that, although in other areas of the curriculum teachers might encourage students to take time to develop their own thinking, in language education what frequently seems to be wanted is talk – plenty of it, and right away.

But it is a curious and perhaps even cruel paradox that in second language classrooms where the explicitly stated (or implicitly understood) goal is production, production and more production, silence can be pedagogically imposed on a learner. This can happen in many ways: by heavily privileging a language in which an individual is not yet capable of self-expression (or worse, by ignoring or forbidding use of any language other than that of the mainstream); by wounding the self-concept of a student who lacks standard pronunciation; by relying exclusively on pedagogical techniques, such as rote drills and memorisation of forms, that might limit the creative and self-affirming impulses of language behaviour; and, ironically, by forcing speech production in the target language in a student who might not be ready for it.

Of course learning environments act on learners in many ways, not all of them, thankfully, as foreboding or potentially destructive as those enumerated above. It would be of considerable interest indeed to explore the question of learning context in relation to various kinds of learner silence. What, for example, might be the correlation between formal (i.e. classroom) and informal learning contexts and the occurrence, or the learner's subjective experience, of silence? And might certain pedagogical approaches, such as the learner-autonomy framework described above with its demands for a re-conceptualisation of the roles of teachers and learners, or even a more general learner-centred praxis, have an impact on the occurrence of silence as a part of the learning process?

If so, what might that impact be, and what new questions would such a study raise? For example, it is one thing to ask whether, in a case where a learner's silence in a language class is due to the fear of being continually corrected, a pedagogy that allowed that student to learn without worry about ongoing correction might reduce silence. It may be another matter, however, to ask whether a particular pedagogy could, of itself, result in less of the kinds of silence I have been considering here. Such silences may be understood as grounded in the individual's unconscious, activated in the language–learning relationship, and symptomatic of a kind of fear not of *making* but rather, in a profound psychical sense, of *being* a mistake (though it must be granted that, seen psychoanalytically, the two are not unrelated). And it would be something else altogether to pose the question of whether less silence would necessarily be an indicator of the absence of psychical conflict and ambivalence within the learner.

What is clear from the present discussion is that curricular and community demands, individual perceptions, intra-personal processes, pedagogical philosophies and ideologies, and personal beliefs about learning and about what matters in learning and in teaching, along with actual classroom practices, are mutually informed, constructed by and through the complex relations of all the participants in education. For individual teachers to challenge these vast constructs requires not only the conviction that to do so is proper, but an understanding of and commitment to a pedagogy whose operating principle is much less one of certainty, and whose scripted role much less that of master, than has traditionally been the case.

Such a challenge might also demand looking on teaching and learning as being less about mastery, either of the self, or of the 'subject', or of the self-*as*-subject (Kaplan, 1993), than about working through the vicissitudes of making and re-making both self and subject. Such a pedagogy might demand that, rather than insisting on certain forms of participation, teachers ask (and indeed be empowered to ask) 'the open-minded questions, the mirroring questions, the benevolently interested questions: What have we here? How can we respond to it genuinely? How can we help it along?' that Roy Schafer suggests offer the potential for genuine dialogue between individuals (Schafer, 1992: 11).

But what kinds of answers can there be to questions like 'what have we here?' when they are met with silence? Common-sense educational discourse often privileges personal information that teachers acquire or are given about their students' personal lives (ethnicity, socio-economic class, family status and so on) as the kind of knowledge likely to be instructive for the development of programs and practices that will meet those students' needs as their teachers perceive them (see Lotherington *et al.*, 2000). And so, in addition to working within a system whose assessment requirements demand measurable products, educators faced with a lack of language production (in the form of silence) might well believe that they must determine the meaning of the very particular silences of individual students in order to find ways to respond to and eliminate them. In her memoir, Alice Kaplan (1993: 174) asks, 'What do students need to know about their teachers?' We might equally ask what teachers ought to know about their students.

This question of the personal – and personal knowledge – in learning is a tricky one: questions concerning the usefulness of such knowledge are trickier still. Certainly there is more than one *kind* of knowledge that a teacher might conceivably need or want to acquire about her students. In addition to what might be termed functional, logistical or administratively-oriented knowledge, and knowledge (mentioned above) relating to socio-economic status and home culture, we might imagine that the inner intellectual and emotional life of each student in a class might be known – or knowledge of it might be desired, to a considerable extent, or not at all, or to any degree in between. But recalling the Winnicottian concept of the secret self (Pitt, 2000: 65), as well as the overarching psychoanalytic concept of the unconscious as always present but rarely accessible to the conscious mind, and adding to that mix the lived experience of the second-language learner, caught for a time between two tongues, in a sense holding her or his tongue in both languages but adequately held by neither, is to render even more bewildering the question of who in reality can know what, and about whom.

How, for example, can teachers know, at any given moment, why some students in the process of acquiring a second language are silent, and what the precise nature of that silence might be? How can they learn this from their students if their students will not, or cannot, tell? And how can they know whether the *not*-telling is grounded in a linguistically-grounded inability or a psychically-informed refusal to tell? Ultimately, how can they know, as Winnicott says they must, 'when they are concerned *not with teaching their subject* but with psychotherapy'? (Winnicott, 1963a, 63; italics in original).

I have argued that language itself is a methodology, as well as a knowledge. It is also implicated, as both knowledge and methodology, in what Pitt (2000: 68) calls 'mak[ing] sense of ourselves in ways that give meaning to our lives ... [and making] relations with others', a part of which must surely be to speak to oneself and to others about the sense that we have made. In the particular case of the language learner 'lost in translation' (Hoffman, 1989), however, there is a temporary loss of both knowledge and methodology. So the language learner's self must try to tell that self *to* itself, and to the world outside itself, in an idiom she does not know and which, at the same time, is trying to translate her, to shift her into the new idiom. Always subject, of course, to the degree to which an individual wants, needs, or is in any sense able to share it, such knowledge is, arguably, unlikely to be readily attained from a second-language learner struggling with language and with identity. Two centuries ago William Wordsworth (1800) recognised, in a note to his poem *The Thorn*, 'the deficiencies of language' that accompany the desire to 'communicate impassioned feelings.' Phillips (1999) maps these deficiencies, and our awareness of them, onto children in the process of acquiring a first language. The invitation he offers, in the form of a hint, is that 'psychoanalysis is one way of speaking up for our formative linguistic incompetence, for the necessary relationship between our verbal uncertainty and our fluency, for the profit of loss' (Phillips, 1999: 57).

For teachers too, Ehrman and Dörnyei maintain, psychoanalytic theory offers ways to help educators '*make sense* of their [and their students'] experience ... [as well as of] group processes in institutions, including educational ones' (Ehrman & Dörnyei, 1998: 200–201; italics in original). Further, while cautioning that '[d]irect process intervention ... using psychoanalytic insights should be done only by those with proper training' (1998: 201), Ehrman and Dörnyei recommend that a teacher faced with 'intensive unconscious communications that affect the work of the class ... [might use psychoanalytic concepts to] *understand his or her own reaction and 'hot buttons'* (1998: 202; italics in original). They also recognise how, in general, the roles he or she takes up, or refuses, can contribute to, or detract from, healthful and helpful teacher–learner relationships.

But with or without psychoanalysis, for a second-language learner (and by extension for that learner's teacher) the problem may not simply be that the new language cannot communicate passions, nor even that it cannot communicate the self, but that *it cannot even communicate its inability to communicate.* Thus, to reframe once more the question of what teachers *ought* to know about their students might be to ask what they *can* know. In reply to this question, and to Riley's (1999: 10) contention that, in the language-learner/adviser relationship, 'we cannot hope to understand what is going on ... unless we have a clear idea of the identities of the participants involved', I offer two reminders of how difficult it can be to come by a 'clear idea'. First, recalling the notion of the individual's core or secret self as continually engaged in a struggle between the need to remain hidden and the need to make itself known (Pitt, 2000), I maintain that educators simply cannot infer the presence in their students of a de facto desire to reveal the self. And second, even if such an desire could be taken for granted, it would also be crucial to recognise that that learner might not be able to achieve it – that the question a learner might ask, if indeed she or he were able to ask it, might be, How can I tell myself to another, when I cannot even tell myself to me?

The dynamic here is thus doubled. An individual may or may not have the conscious desire, combined with the psychical wherewithal, to reveal his or her identity, or to tell a particular secret, but even desire and ability together may not be enough. One who does have both the conscious wish and the psychical capacity to tell a secret might nevertheless lack the linguistic competence to do so. Two lacks are possible – how can a teacher know in a given situation which, if either, is the case?

The question, writ large, bears asking again. How – and what – can educators, specifically second-language teachers, come to know about their students and those students' needs? Perhaps, given the complexity of silence in second language acquisition, and the complexity of desire and ambivalence in learners, and the further complexity of the lives and the work of educators, such direct knowledge is not possible. And this gives rise to other questions. How can we learn to live with this lack of direct knowledge? How can education tolerate the partiality of what it can know?

If I am, perhaps, a little less hopeful than Riley (1999: 10) about the possibility of obtaining 'a clear idea' of the language learner's identity *from the learner* himself or herself, I am nevertheless convinced that, despite or even through silence, ways can be found into relations between teachers and learners that make both relating and learning possible. We may not have a 'clear idea' about a particular learner, but we do have hints.

Some hints can be taken from memoirs and autobiographical writing of the kind examined in this study, and from interpretations of that writing. The first hint might be a very gentle one, the simple reminder that self-writing gives us of the existence in each individual of a multi-layered inner world, and of the importance of tolerating 'the particular peace its author has made between the individuality of his or her subjectivity and the intersubjective and public character of meaning' (Grumet, 1990: 324). For in the complex daily work of education, with its demands and vicissitudes, and its foregrounding of overtly-manifested and readily-observable learning processes as means to perceptible, tangible, quantifiable products of learning, there is a tendency to abstract the learner's – and the teacher's – less visible, subjective and unconscious experiences. This is simply to say that it is quite a difficult thing to remain mindful of the lives of the persons involved in education. Reading and working with autobiographical writing might be a way for educators, and researchers, and indeed for all participants in education, to begin to 'recover human feeling and motivation for studies of education that [have] become anonymous and quantitative' (Grumet, 1990: 322).

A second hint that might be taken, from reading and perhaps also from writing autobiography and memoir, is a kind of intimation of relatedness, different from generalisation, but offering the possibility of thinking about shared aspects of experience among, in this case, second-language learners. Not certainty, we must remember, but possibility: not that one individual's learning *must*, but that it *might*, be a little like another's. Second-language learners in mid-process may not be able to speak about their experience, and there may be ethical reasons not to demand that they do so, but educators might take hints about those silences from the narratives of others. And those hints, once taken, may give us something to ground our intuition and guide our pedagogy, and allow for the possibility that educators can take care without taking control.

This is a tall pedagogical order indeed, for at times it means that teachers, accustomed to knowing, deciding, and most of all doing, must simply wait and see. But perhaps it also means that second-language teaching need not be quite as delicate a process as petting a porcupine. Referring to Bruno Bettelheim's (1979) essay, *Education and the Reality*

*Principle*, Britzman describes the 'good-enough teacher' (modelled on the Winnicottian concept of the 'good-enough mother') as one who 'must engage the student's capacity for illusion and disillusion, the capacity to express and understand, and the capacity to tolerate times of being misunderstood and not understanding' (Britzman, 1998: 41–42). Along with the kinds of holding that Winnicott (1961, 1970) deems necessary for the development of autonomy, and those which for Ehrman and Dörnyei (1998: 224) characterise successful learning environments by 'permit[ting] the client or student to take the risks needed to explore, make mistakes and learn', perhaps a space can be made in pedagogical discourse for an approach of patient waiting, undertaken by a 'good-enough teacher.'

Such an approach could offer the second-language learner within the education system an 'environmental holding' of an intellectual kind: the recognition of a period of waiting and working through that might, in some learners, be manifested in silence. Here again is a reminder that all the work of education, including second-language teaching and learning, and even silence as part of that process, is both intra-personal and also patently social. It is work that embodies individual pleasures, but also disillusionments, anxieties and conflicts between different parts of the individual, as well as the competing promises, demands, rewards and disappointments of its many institutional and individual participants. It is work undertaken both within and between individuals and the world, the inside and the outside, in all the places and moments in which lives are lived, knowledge made and language learned.

Or not learned – even, sometimes, refused. Here Britzman is helpful, gesturing towards the possibility of thinking about silence in learning as one of 'such familiar survival strategies as slipping between the cracks of attention, doing just enough so as not to draw attention to oneself ... indeed making oneself disappear right before the teacher's eyes' (Britzman, 1998: 24). Such a disappearance may be necessary for some learners as they defend against the potential fragmentation brought about by a reduced ability to speak and to be understood, and work through their ambivalent and conflicting desires, conscious and unconscious, about revealing and concealing their selves. Indeed, seen in this way, that is when it is the self, which makes itself known through language, that must be defended (or defended against), silence may cease to be a problem at all. Rather, it might be understood as a useful methodology for the learner to work through or come to accept what we might tentatively call, following Warner (1981: 23), the 'irreconcilable oppositions' inherent in the liminal state of suspension between two languages and between two linguistic identities.

Of course all of these possibilities are no more than that. They are not, and they never can be, a prescriptive program of classroom strategies. This is because, as any teacher knows, there is no one way to teach, and no one way to learn: no single solution, therefore, can ever be more than partial. Larsen-Freeman and Long's frank acknowledgement concerning the prevalence of contradictory findings in SLA research (Larsen-Freeman & Long's 1991: 206, and see also Chapter 1) is worth repeating – though I would like to add to it one emphatic word: 'Practical implications must therefore *always* remain tenuous at best.'

In the light of that partialness, that tenuousness, silence as a kind of methodology might at times be useful for educators, too. 'The good-enough teacher', writes Britzman (1998: 42), 'must also help herself in tolerating the results of her ... own frustration'. That is to say, while some pedagogies may help alleviate silence, and in so doing make the work of the teacher easier, or tolerable, or in some cases possible at all, it is important to remember that alleviating silence may not always be the most useful (or even a possible) immediate objective for the learner. Put differently, when as teachers we consider how best to motivate learners, we must also attend to moments in the learning process when the question of motivation may simply not be relevant – moments that must be worked through, and for which silence might be the means of that working-through. This may be one of the ways in which learner-centred approaches such as those recommended by the learner autonomy model might be useful – if they can help teachers to understand that both speaking and silence belong, ultimately, to the learner.

Educators might also learn, from those they teach, something of the value of waiting and of silence that Peter Cryle (1997) has encapsulated as, for learners, the 'discipline involved in lying down, indeed in relaxing, as well as in sitting upright with eyes on the teacher'. The kindergarten teacher whose experience is related at the very beginning of this book, whose pupil's long silence ended with the sight of a familiar animal, knew the importance of respecting that boy's silence and of waiting for him to be ready to speak. It may be that teachers, too, need to make what Madeleine Grumet (1988: 88) calls 'a place for themselves where they can find the silence that will permit them to draw their experience and understanding into expression.'

It seems to me that this kind of silence, and more specifically the idea of finding, or deliberately making, this kind of silent period, is a silence that opens up rather than shuts down – a silence that might hint at a way of thinking about learning not only a new language as such, but also other kinds of knowledge. For losses as well as gains are a part not only of language learning, but also of the process of acquiring new knowledge or of

learning a new theory, either of which can insist upon a psychical movement as well as a conscious intellectual shift into a new theoretical language
and the corresponding theoretical milieu. As Eva Hoffman discovered, it is
not enough just to learn the new words; one must learn the new world as
well. And at different times and in different contexts, we all have to do this.
Certainly there is a sense in which this book is telling the story of a kind of
language learning, for implicit in the work of triangulating several theoretical discourses is the task of making each of them speak to the others. I have
attempted to negotiate a kind of conversation between psychoanalytic
theory, social theory and SLA research, and in turn to weave that conversation into a dialogue with the narrative texts that seem so compelling – a new
theoretical language, a new conversation.

I wonder whether, in this negotiation, this conversation, there might
perhaps also be something that hints at some of the larger questions that
relate not only to language learning but also to other kinds of learning that
may interfere with individuals in profound and even disturbing ways.
How do we learn? How do we give voice to our learning? And how do we
tolerate learning, what do we do with the problem of articulating learning,
when it is just too hard? It is subtle, this kind of educative hint that the
concept of silence might provide concerning ways of thinking about
learning theory, for example, or about theorising learning. But even so, like
the kind of 'education through hinting, about hinting' that Phillips calls
psychoanalysis, such hints might act as a hopeful '... kind of go-between
between teaching and seduction, sustaining both a complicity and a difference' (Phillips, 1999: 109) – embodying, in other words, their own conflicts,
their own ambivalence, and their own irreconcilable oppositions, but also,
as psychoanalysis keeps insisting, their own wishes and desires.

# References

Bailey, K.M. (1979) An introspective analysis of an individual's language learning experience. In S.D. Krashen and R.C. Scarcella (eds) *Research in Second Language Acquisition: Selected Papers of the Los Angeles Second Language Research Forum* (pp. 58–65). Rowley, MA: Newbury House.

Bailey, K.M. (1983) Competitiveness and anxiety in adult second language learning: Looking *at* and *through* the diary studies. In H.W. Seliger and M.H. Long (eds) *Classroom Oriented Research in Second Language Acquisition* (pp. 67–103). Rowley, MA: Newbury House.

Bailey, K.M. (1991) Diary studies of classroom language learning: The doubting game and the believing game. In E. Sadtono (ed.) *Language Acquisition and the Second/Foreign Language Classroom* (pp. 60–102). Singapore: SEAMEO Regional Language Centre.

Bailey, K.M. and Nunan, D. (eds) (1996) *Voices from the Language Classroom: Qualitative Research in Second Language Education.* Cambridge: Cambridge University Press.

Barthes, R. (1978) *A Lover's Discourse: Fragments* (R. Howard, trans.). New York: Hill and Wang.

Beebe, L.M. (1983) Risk-taking and the language learner. In H.W. Seliger and M.H. Long (eds) *Classroom Oriented Research in Second Language Acquisition* (pp. 39–65). Rowley, MA: Newbury House.

Belcher, D. and Connor, U. (2001) *Reflections on Multiliterate Lives.* Clevedon: Multilingual Matters.

Benson, P. and Voller, P. (eds) (1997) *Autonomy and Independence in Language Learning.* New York: Addison Wesley Longman.

Bettelheim, B. (1979) Education and the reality principle. In *Surviving and Other Essays* (pp. 127–41). New York: Vantage Books.

Bloom, L.R. (1998) *Under the Sign of Hope: Feminist Methodology and Narrative Interpretation.* Albany: State University of New York Press.

Britzman, D.P. (1998) *Lost Subjects, Contested Objects: Toward a Psychoanalytic Inquiry of Learning.* Albany: State University of New York Press.

Britzman, D.P. and Pitt, A.J. (2000) Speculations on difficult knowledge: The project, the protocol, the interviews. Paper presented at the 2000 American Education Research Association Conference, New Orleans.

Brodkey, L. (1996) *Writing Permitted in Designated Areas Only.* Minneapolis: University of Minnesota Press.

Brown, H.D. (1994a) *Principles of Language Learning and Teaching* (3rd edn). Englewood Cliffs, NJ: Prentice-Hall.

Brown, H.D. (1994b) *Teaching by Principles: An Interactive Approach to Language Pedagogy.* Englewood Cliffs, NJ: Prentice Hall Regents.

Brumfit, C., Moon, J. and Tongue, R. (eds) (1991) *Teaching English to Children: From Practice to Principle*. London: Harper Collins.

Burkitt, I. (1991) *Social Selves: Theories of the Social Formation of Personality*. London: Sage Publications.

Carlyle, T. (1907) *Critical and Miscellaneous Essays* (Vol. 4). London: Chapman and Hall.

Chamoiseau, P. (1997) *School Days* (L. Coverdale, trans.). Lincoln: University of Nebraska Press.

Chomsky, N. (1972) *Language and Mind* (revised edn). New York: Harcourt Brace Jovanovich.

Cioran, E.M. (1991) *Anathemas and Admirations* (R. Howard, trans.). New York: Arcade.

Coles, R. (1989) *The Call of Stories: Teaching and the Moral Imagination*. Boston: Houghton Mifflin.

Cotterall, S. and Crabbe, D. (eds) (1999) *Learner Autonomy in Language Learning: Defining the Field and Effecting Change* (pp. 3–9). Frankfurt am Main: Peter Lang.

Courchêne, R. (1992) A comprehension-based approach to curriculum design. In R.J. Courchêne, J.J. Glidden, J. St. John and C. Thérien (eds) *Comprehension-based Second Language Teaching* (pp. 95–117). Ottawa: University of Ottawa Press.

Crabbe, D. (1999) Introduction to Part I: Defining the field. In S. Cotterall and D. Crabbe (eds) *Learner Autonomy in Language Learning: Defining the Field and Effecting Change* (pp. 3–9). Frankfurt am Main: Peter Lang.

Cryle, P. (1997) Kama Sutra and curriculum. Invited paper presented at the Pedagogy and the Body Conference, QueenslandUniversity of Technology, Brisbane. Cited in E. McWilliam (1999) *Pedagogical Pleasures*. New York: Peter Lang.

Curran, C.A. (1972) *Counseling Learning: A Whole-Person Model for Education*. New York: Grune and Stratton.

Dewey, J. (1956) *The Child and the Curriculum, and The School and Society*. Chicago: University of Chicago Press

Dulay, H.C., Burt, M.K. and Krashen, S.D. (1982) *Language Two*. New York: Oxford University Press.

Ehrman, M.E. and Dörnyei, Z. (1998) *Interpersonal Dynamics in Second Language Education: The Visible and Invisible Classroom*. Thousand Oaks: Sage Publications.

Elbow, P. (1973) *Writing without Teachers*. New York: Oxford University Press.

Ellis, R. (1989) Classroom learning styles and their effect on second language acquisition: A study of two learners. *System* 17 (2), 249–62.

Ellis, R. (1996) *The Study of Second Language Acquisition*. Hong Kong: Oxford University Press.

Ely, C.M. (1986) An analysis of discomfort, risktaking, sociability and motivation in the L2 classroom. *Language Learning* 36, 1–25.

Feldstein, R., Fink, B. and Jaanus, M. (eds) (1996) *Reading Seminars I and II: Lacan's Return to Freud: Seminar I, Freud's Papers on Technique; Seminar II, The Ego in Freud's Theory and in the Technique of Psychoanalysis*. Albany: State University of New York Press.

Felman, S. (1993) *What Does a Woman Want? Reading and Sexual Difference*. Baltimore and London: Johns Hopkins University Press.

Fink, B. (1995) *The Lacanian Subject: Between Language and Jouissance*. Princeton, NJ: Princeton University Press.

Fink, B. (1996) The subject and the Other's desire. In R. Feldstein, B. Fink and M. Jaanus (eds) *Reading Seminars I and II: Lacan's Return to Freud: Seminar I, Freud's Papers on Technique; Seminar II, The Ego in Freud's Theory and in the Technique of Psychoanalysis* (pp. 76–97). Albany, NY: State University of New York Press.

Frawley, W. and Lantolf, J.P. (1984) Speaking and self-order: A critique of traditional second language research. *Studies in Second Language Acquisition* 6 (2), 146–59.

Freire, P. (1970) *Pedagogy of the Oppressed*. New York: Herder and Herder.

Freud, A. (1974) *The Writings of Anna Freud* (Vol. 1). New York: International Universities Press.

Freud, S. (1909) Family romances. *The Standard Edition of the Complete Psychological Works of Sigmund Freud* (Vol. 9, pp. 235–41). London: Hogarth Press.

Freud, S. (1911) Formulations on the two principles of mental functioning. In *The Penguin Freud Library* (Vol. 11, pp. 29–44). London: Penguin Books.

Freud, S. (1915a) Instincts and their vicissitudes. In *The Penguin Freud Library* (Vol. 11, pp. 113–38). London: Penguin Books.

Freud, S. (1915b) The unconscious. In *The Penguin Freud Library* (Vol. 11, pp. 167–227). London: Penguin Books.

Freud, S. (1915c) Repression. In *The Penguin Freud Library* (Vol. 11, pp. 141–55). London: Penguin Books.

Freud, S. (1917) Mourning and melancholia. In *The Penguin Freud Library* (Vol. 11, pp. 245–68). London: Penguin Books.

Freud, S. (1925) Negation. In *The Penguin Freud Library* (Vol. 11, pp. 435–42). London: Penguin Books.

Freud, S. (1948) *Inhibitions, Symptoms and Anxiety*. London: Hogarth Press.

Freud, S. (1968) *The Standard Edition of the Complete Psychological Works of Sigmund Freud* (Vol. 9; J. Strachey, trans. and ed.). London: Hogarth Press.

Freud, S. (1991) *The Penguin Freud Library* (Vol. 11): *On Metapsychology: The Theory of Psychoanalysis* (J. Strachey, trans. and ed.). London: Penguin Books.

Gardner, R.C. and Lambert, W.E. (1972) *Attitudes and Motivation in Second-Language Learning*. Rowley, MA: Newbury House.

Gardner, R.C. (1985) *Social Psychology and Second Language Learning: The Role of Attitudes and Motivation*. London: Edward Arnold.

Gee, J.P. (1992) *The Social Mind: Language, Ideology, and Social Practice*. New York: Bergin and Garvey.

Gibbons, J.P. (1985) The silent period: An examination. *Language Learning* 35 (2), 255–67.

Grumet, M.R. (1988) *Bitter Milk: Women and Teaching*. Amherst: University of Massachusetts Press.

Grumet, M.R. (1990) Retrospective: Autobiography and the analysis of educational experience. *Cambridge Journal of Education* 20 (3), 321–35.

Guiora, A.Z., Brannon, R.C. and Dull, C.Y. (1972) Empathy and second language learning. *Language Learning* 22 (1), 111–30.

Hakuta, K. (1976) A case study of a Japanese child learning English as a second language. *Language Learning* 26 (2), 321–51.

Hanania, E.A.S. and Gradman. H.L. (1977) Acquisition of English structures: A case study of an adult native speaker of Arabic in an English-speaking environment. *Language Learning* 27 (1), 75–91.

Harder, P. (1980) Discourse as self-expression: On the reduced personality of the second-language learner. *Applied Linguistics* 1 (3), 262–70.

Harley, B. (1986) *Age in Second Language Acquisition.* Clevedon: Multilingual Matters.

Harré, R. (1993) *Social Being* (2nd edn). Oxford: Blackwell.

Harré, R. and Gillett, G. (1994) *The Discursive Mind.* Thousand Oaks: Sage Publications.

Heilbrun, C.G. (1999) *Women's Lives: The View from the Threshold.* Toronto: University of Toronto Press.

Hoffman, E. (1989) *Lost in Translation: A Life in a New Language.* New York: Penguin Books.

Holec, H. (1981) *Autonomy and Foreign Language Learning.* Oxford: Pergamon.

Hollway, W. and Jefferson, T. (2000) *Doing Qualitative Research Differently: Free Association, Narrative and the Interview Method.* London, Thousand Oaks, New Delhi: Sage Publications.

Howell, S. (1988) From child to human: Chewong concepts of self. In G. Jahoda and I.M. Lewis (eds) *Acquiring Culture: Cross-Cultural Studies in Child Development* (pp. 147–68). London: Routledge.

Huang, J. (1970) A Chinese child's acquisition of English syntax. MA thesis, University of California at Los Angeles.

Huang, J. and Hatch, E. (1978) A Chinese child's acquisition of English. In E. Hatch (ed.) *Second Language Acquisition: A Book of Readings* (pp. 118–31). Rowley, MA: Newbury House.

Huxley, A. (1978) *Point Counter Point.* London: Granada.

Illich, I. (1971) *Deschooling Society.* New York: Harper and Row.

Isson, L., Kjisik, F. and Nordlund, J. (1997) Ten aspects of autonomy. Excerpt from *From Here to Autonomy.* Helsinki: Helsinki University Press. Online document: http://www.helsinki.fi/kksc/alms/tenasp.html.

Jones, R.A. (1977) Psychological, social and personal factors in second language acquisition. MA thesis, University of California at Los Angeles.

Juliá, M. (2001) A professional academic life in two languages. In D. Belcher and U. Connor (eds) *Reflections on Multiliterate Lives.* Clevedon: Multilingual Matters.

Kaplan, A. (1993) *French Lessons.* Chicago: University of Chicago Press.

Kelly, G.A. (1963) *A Theory of Personality: The Psychology of Personal Constructs.* New York: W.W. Norton.

Krashen, S.D. (1982) *Principles and Practice in Second Language Acquisition.* Oxford: Pergamon.

Krashen, S.D. (1985) *The Input Hypothesis: Issues and Implications.* London: Longman.

Laplanche, J. and Pontalis, J.B. (1973) *The Language of Psycho-analysis.* New York: W.W. Norton.

Larsen-Freeman, D. (1983) Second language acquisition: Getting the whole picture. In K.M. Bailey, M.H. Long and S. Peck (eds) *Second Language Acquisition Studies: Selected Papers of the Third Los Angeles Second Language Research Forum* (pp. 3–22). Rowley, MA: Newbury House.

Larsen-Freeman, D. and Long, M.H. (1991) *An Introduction to Second Language Acquisition Research.* London: Longman.

Lehtonen, J. and Sajavaara, K. (1985) The silent Finn. In D. Tannen and M. Saville-Troike (eds) *Perspectives on Silence* (pp. 193–201). Norwood, NJ: Ablex.

Leichman, H. (1977) A diary of one person's acquisition of Indonesian. Unpublished manuscript, University of California, Los Angeles. Cited in K.M. Bailey (1983) Competitiveness and anxiety in adult second language learning: Looking *at* and *through* the diary studies. In H.W. Seliger and M.H. Long (eds) *Classroom Oriented Research in Second Language Acquisition* (pp. 67–103). Rowley, MA: Newbury House.

Lemke, J.L. (1995) *Textual Politics: Discourse and Social Dynamics*. Washington: Taylor and Francis.

Lenneberg, E.H. (1962) Understanding language without ability to speak: A case report. *Journal of Abnormal and Social Psychology* 65, 419–25.

Lévi-Strauss, C. (1987) *Introduction to the Work of Marcel Mauss* (F. Baker, trans.). London: Routledge & Kegan Paul.

Lightbown, P.M. and Spada, N. (1996) *How Languages are Learned*. Hong Kong: Oxford University Press.

Little, D. (1991) *Learner Autonomy I: Definitions, Issues and Problems*. Dublin: Authentik.

Little, D. (1999) Learner autonomy is more than a Western cultural construct. In S. Cotterall and D. Crabbe (eds) *Learner Autonomy in Language Learning: Defining the Field and Effecting Change* (pp. 11–18). Frankfurt am Main: Peter Lang.

Little, D. and Dam, L. (1998) Learner autonomy: What and why? Online document: http://langue.hyper.chubu.ac.jp/jalt/pub/tlt/98/nov/littledam.html

Lotherington, H., Morbey, M.L., Granger, C.A. and Doan, L. (2001) Tearing down the walls: New literacies and new horizons in the elementary school. In *Technology, Teaching and Learning: Issues in the Integration of Technology* (pp. 131–61). Calgary: Detselig.

MacIntyre, P.D. and Gardner, R.C. (1991) Methods and results in the study of foreign language anxiety: A review of the literature. *Language Learning* 41, 25–57.

MacLennan, B.W. and Dies, K.R. (1992) *Group Counseling and Psychotherapy with Adolescents* (2nd edn). New York: Columbia University Press.

Mandelbaum, D.G. (ed.) (1949) *The Selected Writings of Edward Sapir in Language, Culture, and Personality*. Berkeley: University of California Press.

McLaughlin, B. (1978) The monitor model: Some methodological considerations. *Language Learning* 28, 309–332.

Mead, G.H. (1934) *Mind, Self, and Society From the Standpoint of a Social Behaviorist* (C.W. Morris, ed.). Chicago and London: University of Chicago Press.

Miller, G. (1970) Foreword to R. Weir's *Language in the Crib*. The Hague: Mouton.

Miller, J. (1983) *Many Voices: Bilingualism, Culture, and Education*. London: Routledge & Kegan Paul.

Mitchell, R. and Myles, F. (1998) *Second Language Learning Theories*. London: Arnold.

Montessori, M. (1964) *The Montessori Method* (A.E. George, trans.). New York: Schocken Books

Moore, T. (1977) An experimental language handicap (personal account). *Bulletin of the British Psychological Society* 30, 107–110.

Mowrer, D. (1950) *Learning Theory and Personality Dynamics*. New York: Ronald Press.

Muñoz-Duston, E. and Kaplan, J.D. (1985) A sampling of sources on silence. In D. Tannen and M. Saville-Troike (eds) *Perspectives on Silence* (pp. 235–42). Norwood, NJ: Ablex.

Naiman, N., Fröhlich, M., Stern, H. and Todesco, A. (1978) The good language learner. *Research in Education Series No. 7.* Toronto: Ontario Institute for Studies in Education.

National Association for the Education of Young Children (NAYEC) (1995) Position statement: Responding to linguistic and cultural diversity: Recommendations for effective early childhood education. Online document: http://www.ncbe. gwu.edu/miscpubs/naeyc/position.htm.

Nwoye, G. (1985) Eloquent silence among the Igbo of Nigeria. In D. Tannen and M. Saville-Troike (eds) *Perspectives on Silence* (pp. 185–91). Norwood, NJ: Ablex.

Oller, J. (1979) Research on the measurement of affective variables: Some remaining questions. Paper presented at the Colloquium on Second Language Acquisition and Use under Different Circumstances, 1979 TESOL Convention, Boston.

Ontario Ministry of Education and Training (1999a) *The Ontario Curriculum, Grades 9 and 10: French as a Second Language: Core, Extended and Immersion French.* Toronto: Queen's Printer.

Ontario Ministry of Education and Training (1999b) *The Ontario Curriculum, Grades 9 to 12: English as a Second Language and English Literacy Development.* Online document: http://www.edu.gov.on.ca/eng/document/curricul/secondary/ esl/eslful.html#eslprog

Overing, J. (1988) Personal autonomy and the domestic self in Piaroa society. In G. Jahoda and I.M. Lewis (eds) *Acquiring Culture: Cross-Cultural Studies in Child Development* (pp. 169–92). London: Routledge.

Oxford, R. (1992) Who are our students? A synthesis of foreign and second language research on individual differences with implications for instructional practice. *TESL Canada Journal* 90 (2), 30–49. Cited in R. Ellis (1996) *The Study of Second Language Acquisition.* Hong Kong: Oxford University Press.

Parkinson, B. and Howell-Richardson, C. (1989) Learner diaries. In C. Brumfit and R. Mitchell (eds) *Research in the Language Classroom; ELT Documents* 133 (pp. 128–40).

Philip, M.N. (1989) *She Tries her Tongue, her Silence Softly Breaks: Poems.* Charlotte-town, PEI: Ragweed Press.

Phillips, A. (1999) *The Beast in the Nursery: On Curiosity and Other Appetites.* New York: Vintage.

Pitt, A.J. (2000) Hide and seek: The play of the personal in education. *Changing English: Studies in Reading and Culture* 7 (1), 65–74.

Pitt, A.J. and Britzman, D.P. (forthcoming) Speculations on qualities of difficult knowledge in teaching and learning: An experiment in psychoanalytic research. *International Journal of Qualitative Studies in Education.*

Plummer, D. (1976) A summary of a foreign language learning diary. Unpublished manuscript, University of California, Los Angeles. Cited in K.M. Bailey (1983) Competitiveness and anxiety in adult second language learning: Looking *at* and *through* the diary studies. In H.W. Seliger and M.H. Long (eds) *Classroom Oriented Research in Second Language Acquisition* (pp. 67–103). Rowley, MA: Newbury House.

Pontalis, J.B. (1993) *Love of Beginnings* (J. Green and M. Reguis, trans.). New York: Columbia University Press.

Riessman, C.K. (1993) *Narrative Analysis.* Newbury Park, CA: Sage Publications.

Riley, P. (1991) What's your background? The culture and identity of the bilingual child. In C. Brumfit, J. Moon and R. Tongue (eds) *Teaching English to Children: From Practice to Principle*. (pp. 275–88) London: Harper Collins.

Riley, P. (1997) The guru and the conjurer: Aspects of counselling for self-access. In P. Benson and P. Voller (eds) *Autonomy and Independence in Language Learning* (pp. 114–31). New York: Addison Wesley Longman.

Riley, P. (1999) On the social construction of 'the learner'. In S. Cotterall and D. Crabbe (eds) *Learner Autonomy in Language Learning: Defining the Field and Effecting Change* (pp. 29–39). Frankfurt: Peter Lang.

Robinson, P. (1996) *Consciousness, Rules and Instructed Second Language Acquisition*. New York: Peter Lang.

Rodriguez, R. (1988) *Hunger of Memory: The Education of Richard Rodriguez*. New York: Bantam.

Rogers, C.R. (1995) *On Becoming a Person: A Therapist's View of Psychotherapy*. New York: Houghton and Mifflin (first published 1961).

Rose, J. (1984) *The Case of Peter Pan, or, The Impossibility of Children's Fiction*. London: Macmillan.

Sapir, E. (1929) The status of linguistics as a science. *Language* 5, 207–14. Reprinted in D.G. Mandelbaum (1949) *The Selected Writings of Edward Sapir in Language, Culture, and Personality*. Berkeley: University of California Press.

Saunders, G.R. (1985) Silence and noise as emotion management styles: An Italian case. In D. Tannen and M. Saville-Troike (eds) *Perspectives on Silence* (pp. 165–83). Norwood, NJ: Ablex.

Saville-Troike, M. (1988) Private speech: Evidence for second language learning strategies during the 'silent period'. *Journal of Child Language* 15, 567–90.

Schafer, R. (1992) *Retelling a Life: Narration and Dialogue in Psychoanalysis*. New York: Basic.

Schmitz, U. (1994) *Eloquent Silence*. Online document: http://www.linse.uni-essen.de/papers/silence.htm.

Schumann, F.C. and Schumann, J.H. (1977) Diary of a language learner: an introspective study of second language learning. In H.D. Brown, R.H. Crymes and C.A. Yorio (eds) *On TESOL '77: Teaching and Learning English as a Second Language: Trends in Research and Practice* (pp. 241–49). Washington: TESOL.

Schumann, J.H. (1997) *The Neurobiology of Affect in Language*. Malden, MA: Blackwell.

Schutz, A. (1964) The stranger: An essay in social psychology. In *Collected Papers II: Studies in Social Theory* (pp. 91–105). The Hague: Martinus Nijhoff.

Scollon, R. and Scollon, S.B.K. (1981) *Narrative, Literacy and Face in Interethnic Communication*. Norwood, NJ: Ablex.

Scovel, T. (1978) The effect of affect on foreign language learning: A review of the anxiety research. *Language Learning* 28, 129–42.

Seliger, H.W. and Long, M.H. (eds) (1983) *Classroom Oriented Research in Second Language Acquisition*. Rowley, MA: Newbury House.

Selinker, L. (1972) Interlanguage. *International Review of Applied Linguistics* 10, 209–230.

Simondon, G. (1992) The genesis of the individual (M. Cohen and S. Kwinter, trans.). *Incorporations: Zone* 6, 296–319.

Skehan, P. (1989) *Individual Differences in Second-Language Learning*. London: Edward Arnold.

Soler, C. (1996) The symbolic order (1). In R. Feldstein, B. Fink and M. Jaanus (eds) *Reading Seminars I and II: Lacan's Return to Freud: Seminar I, Freud's Papers on Technique; Seminar II, The Ego in Freud's Theory and in the Technique of Psychoanalysis* (pp. 39–46). Albany: State University of New York Press.

Söter, A. (2001) Straddling three worlds. In D. Belcher and U. Connor (eds) *Reflections on Multiliterate Lives*. Clevedon: Multilingual Matters.

Standal, S. (1954) The need for positive regard: A contribution to client-centered theory. PhD thesis, University of Chicago. Cited in C. Rogers (1995) *On Becoming a Person: A Therapist's View of Psychotherapy*. New York: Houghton and Miflin.

Steiner, G. (1970) The retreat from the Word. In *Language and Silence: Essays on Language, Literature and the Inhuman* (pp. 12–35). New York: Atheneum.

Tannen, D. and Saville-Troike, M. (1985) *Perspectives on Silence*. Norwood, NJ: Ablex.

Terrell, T. (1977) A natural approach to second language acquisition and learning. *Modern Language Journal* 61, 325–37.

Tsui, A. (1996) Reticence and anxiety in second language learning. In K.M. Bailey and D. Nunan (eds) *Voices from the Language Classroom: Qualitative Research in Second Language Education* (pp. 145–67). Cambridge: Cambridge University Press.

Ushioda, E. (1996) *Learner Autonomy 5: The Role of Motivation*. Dublin: Authentik.

Voller, P. (1997) Does the teacher have a role in autonomous language learning? In P. Benson and P. Voller (eds) *Autonomy and Independence in Language Learning* (pp. 98–113). New York: Addison Wesley Longman.

Vygotsky, L. (1997) *Thought and Language* (A. Kozulin, trans. and ed.). Cambridge, MA: MIT Press.

Walsleben, M. (1976) Cognitive and affective factors influencing a learner of Persian (Farsi) including a journal of second language acquisition. Unpublished manuscript, University of California, Los Angeles. Cited in K.M. Bailey (1983) Competitiveness and anxiety in adult second language learning: Looking at and through the diary studies. In H.W. Seliger and M.H. Long (eds) *Classroom Oriented Research in Second Language Acquisition* (pp. 67–103). Rowley, MA: Newbury House.

Warner, M. (1981) *Joan of Arc: The Image of Female Heroism*. London: Weidenfeld & Nicolson.

Weir, R.H. (1970) *Language in the Crib*. The Hague: Mouton.

Whorf, B.L. (1956) *Language, Thought and Reality: Selected Writings of Benjamin Lee Whorf* (ed. J.B. Carroll). Cambridge, MA: MIT Press.

Winnicott, D.W. (1961) Varieties of psychotherapy. In *Home is Where We Start From: Essays by a Psychoanalyst* (pp. 101–11). New York: W.W. Norton.

Winnicott, D.W. (1963a) Sum, I am. In *Home is Where We Start From: Essays by a Psychoanalyst* (pp. 55–64). New York: W.W. Norton.

Winnicott, D.W. (1963b) The value of depression. In *Home is Where We Start From: Essays by a Psychoanalyst* (pp. 71–79). New York: W.W. Norton.

Winnicott, D.W. (1965) *The Maturational Processes and the Facilitating Environment: Studies in the Theory of Emotional Development*. Madison, CT: International Universities Press.

Winnicott, D.W. (1965) Communicating and not communicating leading to a study of certain opposites. In *The Maturational Processes and the Facilitating Environment: Studies in the Theory of Emotional Development* (pp. 170–92). Madison, CT: International Universities.

Winnicott, D.W. (1967) The concept of a healthy individual. In *Home is Where We Start From: Essays by a Psychoanalyst* (pp. 21–38). New York; London: W.W. Norton.

Winnicott, D.W. (1970) Cure. In *Home is Where We Start From: Essays by a Psychoanalyst* (pp.112–20). New York: W.W. Norton.

Winnicott, D.W. (1990) *Home is Where We Start From: Essays by a Psychoanalyst*. New York: W.W. Norton.

Winnicott, D.W. (1996) *Thinking about Children*. Reading, MA: Addison-Wesley.

Wittgenstein, L. (1921) *Tractatus Logico-Philosophicus*, Section 7 (D.F. Pears and B.F. McGuinness, trans.). London: Routledge & Kegan Paul, 1974.

Wolfe, D.M. and Kolb, D.A. (1984) Career development, personal growth, and experiential learning. In D.A. Kolb, I.M. Rubin and J.M. McIntyre (eds) *Organizational Psychology: Readings on Human Behavior in Organizations* (4th edn, pp. 124–52). Englewood Cliffs, NJ: Prentice-Hall.

Wordsworth, W. (1800) Note to the thorn. In J. Butler and K. Green (eds) *Lyrical Ballads, and Other Poems, 1797–1800*. Ithaca, NY: Cornell University Press, 1992.

Wu, Z. (1993) Language, consciousness and personal growth: An autobiographic study of a second language learner. PhD thesis, University of Alberta.

Young, D. (1986) The relationship between anxiety and foreign language oral proficiency. *Foreign Language Annals* 19, 439–45.

# Index

135

UNIVERSITY LIBRARY
3 8062 00500 1819